The art of flower arrangement came to Japan, via Korea, from China. The ground
had been prepared, as Japanese painters had already adopted many traditional Chinese
techniques. From this a style of flower painting burgeoned and rose to superb heights by the
seventeenth century.

Like the Chinese, the Japanese developed a unique brush technique for water colour on
silk or paper.

With woodblock printing there was a widespread stimulus resulting in the art of flower
arranging taking root and developing with extraordinary vigour as well as an awesome beauty.

So it came about that the interest of eminent men, such as the Japanese national hero,
Hidiyoshi, and the Shogun Ashekaga, was aroused, and the Shogun's Kyoto Palace thus
became the birthplace of Ikebana.

JAPANESE FLOWER ARRANGEMENT

IKEBANA

JOHN MARCH–PENNEY

With Photographs by JANET MARCH-PENNEY

HAMLYN
LONDON · NEW YORK · SYDNEY · TORONTO

Published by
THE HAMLYN PUBLISHING GROUP LIMITED
LONDON · NEW YORK · SYDNEY · TORONTO
Hamlyn House, Feltham, Middlesex, England

FIRST PUBLISHED - 1969
SECOND IMPRESSION, 1973

© The Hamlyn Publishing Group Limited, 1969
Printed in Italy by Arnoldo Mondadori Officine Grafiche - Verona

ISBN 0 600 02111 4

Acknowledgements

I am most grateful for the assistance which I have had from many helpers in producing this book. Some are anonymous, others are specifically mentioned in a footnote.
My gratitude is due to all from whom I have learned about Ikebana. I must mention Mrs. Martha Neese (President of Ikebana International and editor of its magazine) from whose well-researched articles I have received much inspiration and help. Especial thanks are due to my harshest critic, my photographer, whom I drove relentlessly but who has patiently encouraged me throughout the years.

Footnote
My special thanks go to F. W. Erwood of Covent Garden, London and to all friends with gardens who produced branches and flowers; to the firm of G.B.S. Film Lighting of Greenford, Middlesex, who produced photo floods throughout the floral seasons, and Arthur Sanderson and Sons who provided Japanese wallpapers for backgrounds.

Contents

Foreword

It has been said that Japanese Flower Arrangement is not suited to Western homes. There is also the (happily diminishing) insularity which flinches at the mention of a foreign art, and it is now accepted that all media bringing universal aspects of beauty to our homes (and so to our daily lives) are breaking down our anti-cosmopolitan attitudes.

The process started with tea-drinking. It is our national habit to break the working day with welcome pauses. The Orient has long known the virtue of the refreshing cup brewed from that 'Queen of the Camellias', the tea plant. Japan devised the manner of making and drinking it in the perfectionist ritual of the Tea Ceremony.

So let us face facts. The Orient can and does do some things better than we do! This fact, once accepted, prepares us to take a stance of humility and to approach the centuries-old art of Ikebana which, like the Tea Ceremony, is becoming adapted to Western ways of living.

Books on the subject are legion. And how beautiful they are! Every city, town or village has its Flower Club and visiting experts to demonstrate and teach the art. The movement is quite universal, throughout Europe, the Americas and Asia.

A universal 'love of something', must surely contribute to the global peace for which we long. Flower arranging may be ephemeral but it both enlivens our days and beautifies our homes.

Whether we be Christian, Muslim, Buddist, Shintoist, Pagan or Agnostic there is the inescapable and universal truth: *In the beauty of that flower is revealed the hand of the creator.*

1 How do I start?

Fundamental styles and basic arrangements

Ikebana is *not* difficult! Like music, painting and cooking it calls only for the observance of rules and proportions.

Broadly speaking, all Schools in Japan have two fundamental styles: *moribana** or shallow bowl style; *nageire* or tall vase style.

Let us start with the Sogetsu School interpretations, because they are both attractive and easily learned.

Two basic arrangements are suitable for both of the above styles: *risshin kei* or upright arrangements; *keishin kei* or slanting arrangements.

In addition, there is a horizontal arrangement or *heishin kei* with variations, but mastery of the *risshin kei* and *keishin kei* should first be established in the *moribana* style. The upright and slanting arrangements should then be attempted in the *nageire* style. This order is recommended because placement of main branches or stems in *nageire* style requires a little practice, whereas *moribana* style is easier because a *kensan* or pinholder is used.

The Sogetsu School has created eight variations of each basic arrangement, by interchanges of placement for the three stems used — long, medium and short. This gives a field of over thirty different upright and slanting arrangements for the beginner — nine each *risshin kei* in *moribana* and *nageire* styles and similarly for *keishin kei* (see *plates 1, 2, 3*).

It must be stressed, however, that these two basic arrangements and their eight variations in the two fundamental styles are like musical chords and simple exercises. They are attractive in themselves. As well

The two basic styles according to the Sogetsu School.

1 LEFT: *Moribana* style (*risshin kei*) basic upright arrangement. In this arrangement, *shin* and *soe* are branches, but *hikae* is a flower. The curve of *soe* should echo that of *shin*, and if supporting stems are required they are usually placed before and behind the stems they support. *Hikae* might have a supporting flower in front. Avoid hiding the lines of *shin* and *soe* which should appear to be coming from a common parent stem as in a plant. After placing the flowers – which are the heart of and dominate the arrangement – the *kenzan* (in position 1) is hidden by using *tomi*.

2 RIGHT: *Moribana* style (*keishin kei*) basic slanting arrangement. By placing the *kenzan* in position 3 the longest stem leans forward over the water. Note that the change from basic upright to basic slanting arrangement is effected by a transposition of the placement planes for *shin* and *soe* and their positions in the *kenzan*. As the *kenzan* (in position 3) is in full view it must be carefully hidden by *tomi* or forward-leaning supporting stems for *hikae*.

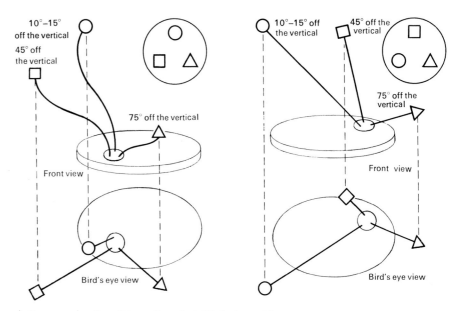

* *For an explanation of terms throughout this book, see Glossary, page 139.*

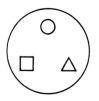 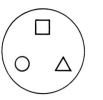

3 The basic styles and the eight variations. *Moribana* style (*risshin kei*) basic upright arrangement. *Soe* 'echoes' the curve of the *shin*, and the *hikae* flower is sometimes supplemented with supporting flowers but the lines of the design should not be lost. *Kenzan* position 1.

Moribana style (*keishin kei*) basic slanting arrangement. *Shin* and *soe* of basic upright *risshin kei* are transposed. *Shin*'s placement plane becomes 45° and that of *soe* 15°. The *hikae* flower is untouched. Fill in flowers are placed between *shin* and *soe* and at the front and side of *hikae*. *Kenzan* position 3, as slanting arrangement looks best leaning over water.

Risshin kei variation 1. *Shin* is moved from left back to right back in the same placement plane. This opens up the space between *shin* and *soe* and thus design is preserved by avoidance of supplemental stems.

Keishin kei variation 1. The placement plane of *soe* is moved from 15° forward to 15° backward slanting.

Risshin kei variation 2. *Soe* and *hikae* are transposed, *shin* remaining as in the basic style. *Soe* takes the *hikae* placement plane of 75°, and *hikae* that of the *soe* placement plane of 45°.

Keishin kei variation 2. The exchange of *soe* from the rear to the *hikae* position in front takes place. *Shin* remains as in basic *keishin kei*.

Variation 5. This is known as the *divided kenzan* or 'double arrangement'. A feeling of space and distance should be apparent. In the *risshin kei* (upright) variation, it must be remembered in doing this that water is part of the design. Usually the larger *kenzan* at front holds *shin* and *soe*, and *hikae* is in the second and smaller *kenzan* at back (*kenzan* position 3). In the *keishin kei* (slanting) variation, the larger *kenzan* is at the back holds *shin* and *soe*, the smaller *kenzan* at front holding *hikae*. The splitting of the *kenzan* can be applied to any of the other variations as well as the basic styles

  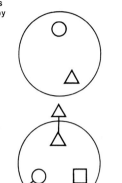

Risshin kei variation 3. The *hikae* takes the same placement plane of 75°, but straight out toward the viewer, while *shin* and *soe* fan out at their appropriate placement planes at the back.

Keishin kei variation 3. *Hikae* is generally a branch instead of a flower as normally. If a flower is chosen for *hikae* it will require supporting flowers. This is often called a three-view arrangement and can be viewed accordingly.

Variation 4 is called the omission style as *soe* is omitted. The two main stems can be of similar material with advantage but dissimilar materials are often used (onion flower and broom). If similar stems are used the enclosing form lines are most attractive being closing (upright) and opening (slanting).

Variation 6 is called the 'flat' or 'horizontal style' and since it may be viewed from four sides it is essentially a table centre arrangement. It does not seem to be Japanese in character except for Western type homes and furnishing in Japan. It is attractive when low-slanting in a shallow bowl but in the upright form it is less popular.

Variation 7 is the triad of arrangements known as *morimono* (or fruit and flowers in a platter or basket), *ukibana* (or floating flowers) and *shikibana* (or flowers placed flat, without *kenzan* or container, in honour of a guest).

Variation 8 is the combination of two containers, or more, having complementary arrangements in them composed of variations or basics in the upright and slanting styles.

as developing skill in seeing and selecting beautiful lines, their continued practice promotes hand and eye co-ordination, and accurate judgement of angles and proportions. Moreover the practice engenders both self-discipline and patience.

Risshin kei or basic upright arrangement
The basic arrangements of main stems are simply the framework or setting for the flowers. Except where a flower is one of the three main stems, placement technique for fill-in flowers is dealt with separately.

For *risshin kei* in both *moribana* and *nageire* styles, the longest stem slants to the left and forward at an angle of 10 to 15 degrees off the vertical, the medium-length stem likewise at 45 degrees and the shortest stem to the right and forward at 75 degress off the vertical. The longest stem should preferably be curved like a bow.

Keishin kei or basic slanting arrangement
For *keishin kei*, both *moribana* and *nageire* styles also have three stems but the longest and medium stems are transposed. The longest stem now slants forward toward the viewer's left shoulder at 45 degrees, while the medium stem replacing it slants at about 15 degrees off the vertical.

Preparation of main stems
The first step is the preparation of the three main stems. In the Sogetsu

6 Pruning. For the sake of clarity leaves are not shown. To reveal an attractive line or curve, surplus material must be pruned away. Avoid a fork tip by cutting off one or other unless they are quite uneven. When pruning, the slanting cut should be made invisible to the viewer by making the longer side toward the front. (A whitish scar is unsightly and should also be rendered invisible by rubbing with a little earth to darken the cut.)

School these are called:

Shin The longest stem. Its symbol ○ suggests the sun in heaven.

Soe The medium stem. Its symbol □ suggests man standing squarely on the earth.

Hikae The shortest stem. Its symbol △ suggests a mountain peak on earth.

(*Shin*, deriving from the ancient *rikka* arrangements, is common to most schools. *Hikae* is called *tai* in the Ikenobo School, which is the most ancient school in Japan and used the terms *shin* and *soe* for the appropriate branches of classical *rikka* in the fifteenth century.)

Preparing the main stems is not difficult if care is taken in the choice of material. Line is important and it should have attractive curves, either naturally or achieved by bending. One soon learns how to prune away ruthlessly the superfluous leaves and branches to reveal the required line (see *plate 6*). One also learns with experience which materials are the most pliable. (For example, pine branches are inclined to be brittle, whereas pussy-willow, oak and broom can be bent to take up a curve quite easily.) The techniques of bending and cutting are explained in detail later. It is important to see that the lower ends of the main stems are trimmed clean for the width of two hands — 6 to 8 inches.

All branches have a right and a wrong side, and in placing them the right side must be toward the viewer — neither profile nor full, but about three-quarter view.

Basic dimensions and proportions

Now let us consider proportions, by which we mean the relative lengths

4 FAR LEFT: Simple *moribana, risshin kei* basic style. *Shin* and *soe* of broom, *hikae* and *jushis* of chrysanthemums, *tomi* of berberis.

5 LEFT: *Risshin kei.* The *shin* stem is of lilies, *soe* and *hikae* of pine. *Tomi* is of pine and lily with bud.

7 BELOW: *Moribana* style. The standard measurement for the longest main stem (*shin*) is the diameter plus height and up to half as much again.

8 RIGHT: *Keishin kei*, slanting style basic. *Shin* and *soe* of bamboo, *hikae* of tawny chrysanthemums. *Jushis* are two flowers and a sprig of bamboo. The container is of carved bamboo.

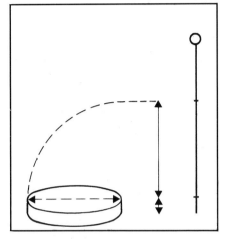

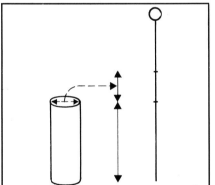

9 *Nageire* style. The standard measurement for the longest main stem (*shin*) is the diameter plus height and as much as half again.

of the three main stems in basic arrangements, whether in *moribana* or *nageire* style.

The length of *shin* is determined by the dimensions of the bowl or vase used, as shown in diagram form in *plates 7* and *9*. We should forget the expression 'near enough'. Until the eye is trained in estimating lengths it is wise to be precise. With a diversity of bowl and vase sizes it has been found an advantage to have large, standard and medium lengths of *shin*.

The diameter-plus-height of the bowl or vase is the basic dimension for all measurements of the main stems. For example, a bowl 10 inches wide and 4 inches tall has a basic dimension of 14 inches. This dimension is used as follows for measuring the length of *shin*:

Large arrangements: twice the basic dimension (in the example, 28 inches).

Standard arrangements: one and a half times the basic dimension (in the example, 21 inches).

Small arrangements: the basic dimension (in the example, 14 inches).

The measurements of medium and short stems are then easily determined, because they are proportions of the *shin* stem used. For all arrangements, *soe* is three-quarters of *shin* in length. In standard and small arrangements, *hikae* should be three-quarters of *soe*. In large arrangements, however, *hikae* should be half of *soe*. Thus, using the basic dimension of 14 inches, *shin* would be 28 inches, *soe* would then be three-quarters of *shin* or 21 inches and *hikae* half of this length. These simple calculations apply to both *moribana* and *nageire*.

An easy way to obtain the basic dimension is to place the tip of the *shin* stem on the table against the vase. Holding the stem upright, place

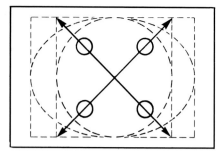

10 Standard positions for *kenzan* in round, square, oval or oblong rectangular bowls; *kenzan* should be moved outward towards rim of bowl, in the direction of axes shown by arrows, for oval, square and rectangular bowls.

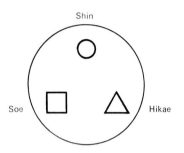

11 Placement positions in *kenzan* for three main stems. Basic *risshin kei* or upright arrangement.

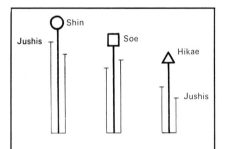

12 According to Sogetsu School, *shin*, *soe* and *hikae* in standard proportions, with supplementary or supporting stems which are called *jushis*, and are different in length and shorter than the stem they supplement. In the diagram two *jushis* are shown with each main stem, but several *jushis* can be used provided they are all of different lengths and always shorter than the stem supported. The use of *jushis* is necessary with slender material such as pussy-willow which might otherwise look sparse and insignificant.

the thumb and forefinger of the free hand on the stem at the rim of the vase. This marker is then lowered across the diameter so that the other hand can hold the stem at the opposite side. Having thus obtained the basic dimension for the vase, the stem lengths can be determined as explained above.

The placing of the kensan in moribana style
In *moribana* arrangements, the position of the *kenzan* is important. The *kenzan* in rarely centred, and the Sogetsu School uses four distinct positions (see *plate 10*). As a rule, the position chosen depends on the season. Rear positions are used for summer, so that viewing the stems reflected in the water suggests coolness. Conversely, the front positions are used in winter. Ikebana not only reflects the seasons but also the way of life at any particular time, such as the annual festivals. The arrangement is the cosmos in miniature, and symbolically the earth may be a field, a hillside, a garden, a pond, the seashore or the fringe of a woodland glade, depending on the materials used. An arrangement should not, however, attempt to represent but rather it should suggest with subtle simplicity. The viewer's imagination must do some work too! For the double *kenzan* arrangement, sometimes called the 'fish-path' arrangement, it would be superfluous to put a goldfish in the bowl!

The *kenzan* was the clever Janapese solution for holding up branches to suggest growth in *moribana* style arrangements. In the *kenzan* itself there are three positions for placement of the main stems, and these are denoted in *plate 11* by the Sogetsu symbols for *shin*, *soe* and *hikae*. The fill-in flowers are placed within these three placement points. They are the heart of the arrangement, like a gem in its setting. The Japanese word for them is *jushis*, and it also includes any supporting stems for the three main stems if the arrangement looks sparse. It should be noted that supporting stems, if used, should always be shorter than the main stems. They should lean towards the viewer, and their placement is no less important than that of the main stems (see *plate 12*).

The three planes of placement for main stems
The angle of slant away from the vertical has been mentioned, but the fact that the angles are set in three different planes should be stressed (see *plate 13*). Most beginners make the mistake of setting the stems at the correct angles but 'fanwise' in the same plane, so that their work looks flat, having no depth. For this reason I have chosen the term 'the three planes of placement' for the main stems. This will be easily understood from the diagrams in *plate 14* of three imaginary cones inverted. I am indebted to Stella Coe for this idea, which she devised for her flower arranging students.

Impaling techinique for all branches and flowers (plates 15-18)
The end to be impaled on the *kenzan* should always be cut at a sharp angle so that the sharp end of the wedge enters between the pins. The branch can then be slanted to give the required plane of placement. Flowers, on the other hand, should always be cut flush to facilitate placement as their stems are usually more fragile. (An exception is the stems of chrysanthemums which are invariably broken, not cut, resulting in a longer life.) Certain succulent stems or soft thick ones call for a stiff stake, one or two inches long, which can be inserted in the *kenzan*. The flower stem can then be fixed over the stake. Hyacinth and amaryllis

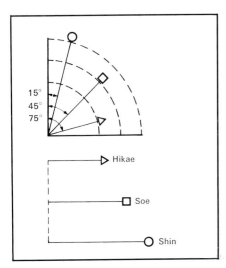

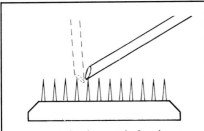

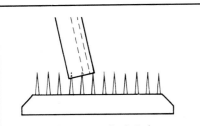

13 Side view of the three main stems showing standard relative proportions and their angles of slant from the vertical (i. e., the three planes of placement). The cosmic significance of an arrangement, heaven, earth and man, while simplified in modern styles, is derived from ancient *rikka* arrangements.

14 RIGHT: Imaginary inverted cones showing the three planes of placement for the three main stems, *moribana* or *nagiere* style.

15 Insert the sharp end of wedge cut between the *kenzan* pins and then bend to required angle.

16 For placement of soft fleshy stems a stake should first be placed firmly in the *kenzan* and the soft stem inpaled on it.

are, for example, best placed this way. Some flower stems, being both slender and soft (like freesias), require a short support. There are several ways of effecting this. The quickest is to cut a 'sock' about two inches long of, say, gladioli or chrysanthemum stem. After making a hole throught the sock, pass the thin stem through the hole before placing the sock on the *kenzan* at the required angle. Soft slender stems like reeds may also be bound together with an elastic band, or tied with raffia. Perhaps a better way of ensuring that water-rising through the stem is not impaired, is to tie in two places an inch or two of stiff stem as a brace. Whatever reinforcement in used, the end of the flower stem must be in water and not pinched.

I have also found that the stems of dried teazles, cut in three-inch lengths, make excellent socks because when dry they are like a thin tube, giving good stability; they are equally suitable as stakes for fleshy stems. Florists' gutta percha tape, in green or natural colouring, is an invaluable aid because it does not require tying. The warmth of the fingers is enough to render it adhesive under gentle pressure, since gutta percha softens at about 90°F.

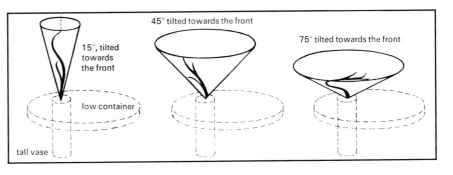

Flower placement

There is art in the placement of flowers when completing an arrangement and it is best to start right, so that the correct way becomes almost automatic. A good practice is to take three flowers, putting them together so that each bloom is below the preceding one but with a little head-room. If the three stems are then cut together we have our three filler-flowers of different lengths, like the main stems. All three should, of course, be shorter than the flower used for the *hikae* main stem, or any supporting stems if they are used.

The medium-length flower should be placed first, leaning forward so that the face of the flower is turned toward the sun in heaven. Next take the longest flower and place it towards *soe*, but always forward and upward looking. The shortest flower is placed at the back at a similar angle. Any number of additional flowers may be used if the arrangement looks 'thin', but none should be longer than the longest flower. Sometimes a very short-stemmed flower is placed at the back of the *kenzan*, low down and barely visible; but its placement there gives an element of surprise. One might call it a 'shadow' but its effect is to give depth to an arrangement.

It is logical that the smallest flower should be the one with the longest stem, because in natural growth the bud is usually found at the top. The largest flower has a medium-length stem, as it is almost in full bloom, while the medium-sized flower with the shortest stem passes the claim for attention to the perfect and largest flower just above it.

Large flowers about four inches across should not be used except for very big arrangements. Ancient tradition stipulated odd numbers of flowers — one, three, five, seven — but this has lapsed along with the inhibition against even numbers and, especially, the use of four flowers. The Japanese word for 'death' is very similar to that for 'four' and for this reason four flowers were considered an ill omen.

At this point it should be mentioned that the ancient books on Ikebana contend that 'the flowers will tell you the way'. The teaching of the correct placement of flowers is based on this concept.

Finishing touches
The finishing touches, which should be made with the arrangement in the position where it is to be displayed, consist of trimming off unsightly or superfluous leaves and hiding the *kenzan*, which should not be visible from a distance of three feet. Very suitable for this purpose are the small branches cut off in pruning *shin* and *soe*, if the leaves are not too big. Stones or pebbles are often used, as is driftwood. It should be remembered that driftwood soaks up water and discolours both itself and the water in the bowl, which is very undesirable. Its positioning thus requires care. The choice of these items, which are called *tomi* in Japanese, is a personal one but it should also depend on the season. Some flower arrangers favour large fleshy leaves because their brilliant green is a foil for the colours of the flowers.

Nageire style, fixing technique for main stems (plates 19-22)
Japanese ingenuity soon found the easiest way to place branches in tall vases, exactly how they wished the branches to stand, whether or not they were top-heavy. All who practice this art soon learn that Ikebana overcomes the obstinacy of material by simplification, in the search for and revelation of beauty.

17 Fixing technique for a tall vase. Standing on the *kenzan*, to hold it upright, is a heavy cleft stick with a pine branch wedged in the cleft and locked with a cleft branch of driftwood. This is an example of the interlocking crotch.

18 Stem passed through teazle ready for impaling on *kenzan*. This is an easy way of handling fragile stems.

Mr. Sofu Teshigahara, Dean of the Sogetsu School in Tokyo, in his recent book, '*Sofu: His Boundless World of Form and Colour*', indicates that in one sense Ikebana is a lie because the intention is not to show how plants and flowers grow. It is rather to create a new beauty by using all elements of nature for making a design.

It follows that no time should be lost in gaining mastery of the simple technique of placing 'difficult' branches securely in a tall vase; otherwise they tend to flop due to gravity. *Nageire* is sometimes called 'thrown in' style. This may be because it is nearly always assymetrical, or possibly because of an ancient story that a certain war-lord once called on his servant to prepare him tea and to do an Ikebana for the refreshment of his spirit. Having no equipment for flower arranging, the servant solved the problem by leaving his knife stuck by the blade in the branch. This device counterbalanced its top weight.

The accompanying diagrams show clearly several ways of obtaining stability by an economy of means — plus a little patience. Patience plays a part because the short pieces of stem cut off to fit the neck of a vase *must* be exact. Obviously one cuts the length approximately at first, afterwards removing the slightest amounts, piece by piece, until the fit is perfect. Cuts are usually at a slant, to fit the curvature of the vase. The fit must be firm enough for a vase to be lifted and held above the table by holding this support. Much time will be saved, and frustration avoided, if one has a session of cutting and fitting the various types of supports. One of the best materials to practice with is willow (no thicker than one's little finger) because of its flexibility. A little 'give' by bending is desirable to ensure a tight fit. Do not force the fit as the neck of the ceramic vase might break. The ancient test for strength is to tap the vase rim lightly with a pencil. A high note is associated with the high temperature firing required for stoneware, which is strong. A low note indicates the lower temperature firing used for ceramic pottery, which is more fragile.

It is probably easiest to start with the 'X' or cross support. Select a stem according to the size of the vase opening. The larger the opening, the stouter should be the stem used. After a trial fit, the cross should be tied or wired at the intersection and then fitted tightly. A branch will then remain stable when resting on the rim of the vase and having its lower end *under* the intersection and balanced against the opposite inside surface of the vase. The end should, of course, be cut at a slant so that it rests flat against the inside of the vase. To ensure water-rising a slit should be cut in the end. This is an easy and very effective way of balancing a branch that must slant low in its placement plane. Branches slanting at only 10 to 45 degrees are placed straight through the required quarter section of the cross and lean against the intersection.

Other traditional devices are the 'Y' or forked twig support. The size of

22 Fixing technique for a heavy branch in a tall vase. This shows the interlocking crotch fixture. The cleft *kubari* is wired to stop complete splitting.

23 *Nageire* arrangement, slanting style, in a tall ceramic by Kay Pritchett. *Shin* and *soe* are mossy apple branches, *hikae* is a blue hyacinth. The second hyacinth and pine are *jushis*.

the fork is gauged for suitability to hold the stems it supports. These stems are held firmly in place with a crossbar (see *plate 22* opposite). The forked twig is called a *kubari* in Japanese and the crossbar is known as an *ichimongi*, but most teachers use the word *kubari* for the fixing arrangement described. These fixing supports are scarcely visible when the vase has had water added, as it should cover the supports.

Using an 'interlocking crotch' support is a satisfactory way of balancing branches which are inclined to be rather top-heavy. It is not suited, however, for material which is brittle, unless great care is exercised and the termination of the split which forms a crotch is wired. If a branch is very heavy, the interlocking crotch will require a crossbar support to keep the interlock in position, unless the interlock comes under the neck of the vase and is held there by it.

Naturally, the pruning of all superfluous leaves and branches attached to a main stem will not only bring out the line but, by lessening the weight, make the fixing easier.

Pine is perhaps one of the most top-heavy branch materials encountered and needs ruthless pruning, not only of branches but all needles that are not young and fresh looking. (An interesting effect may, incidentally, be obtained by giving bunches of needles a 'hair-cut', holding the needles tightly compressed and cutting them to half length.) Pine looks well with most flowers, and particularly with roses or carnations. In Japan, it is combined with bamboo and plum blossom for the traditional New Year arrangements. Symbolically, the strength and long life of the ever-

24 OPPOSITE: Basic upright style
(*risshin kei*). *Shin* and *soe* follow the
same line or curve and are usually branches
of similar material, *hikae* being a flower.
It is essential that these lines stand out
clearly even if supported by supplementary
stems.

25 Upright style variation 1. *Shin* slants
backwards to the right opening up the space
towards *soe*. Any supporting stems
should be rather short so that the
space remains uncluttered.

26 Upright style variation 2. The *shin*
is as in the basic style but
soe and *hikae* are interchanged.

27 Upright style variation 3. Sometimes
called the 'fan' arrangement. Here *hikae*
comes out straight in front while *shin*
and *soe* suggest a fan opening at the back
of it. Similar material is used for all three
stems but *hikae* may be a flower. This
arrangement is possibly a result of the
Western influence, as it is designed for
viewing from three sides and is thus
suited for side tables in Western type
interiors.

28 Upright style variation 4. This is
called the 'style of omission' as *soe* has
been left out. Usually this variation
emphasises movement in the lines or
contrasting masses used, especially if
flowering shrub is used for both *shin*
and *hikae*. It is attractive if the
movement of lines suggests, but does not
complete, an 'enclosing form'.

29 Upright style variation 5. This is called
the divided *kenzan* style because two
kenzans are used, *shin* and *soe* being placed
in one and *hikae* in the other. The water
must be visible as it forms part of the design.

30 Basic slanting style (*keishin kei*). The
slanting styles are effected by an interchange
of *shin* and *soe*. In the upright styles *shin*
usually takes an angle of 15° off the vertical.
In slanting styles it usually takes the 45°
placement angle. *Shin* and *hikae*
thus lean towards the viewer.

31 Slanting style variation 1. In this, *soe*
leans 15° forward and off the vertical.

32 Slanting style variation 2. *Shin* remains
as in the basic slanting style position and
there is an interchange of *soe* and *hikae*
(back and front stems). *Hikae* now leans
toward the left at the back and
15° forward off the vertical.

green pine is linked with the resilience of bamboo, which stands up to
adversity by bending with the wind, while the plum blossom heralds
the welcome Spring. It will be found that a small sprig of pine at the neck
of a tall vase in a *nageire* arrangement can be most effective in giving
interest to the arrangement.

In making the splits for an interlocking crotch, it is wise to 'ring' the
bark of the branch with the scissors where the split is to stop. This is done
by holding the branch firmly between the jaws of the scissors and exerting
light pressure as the branch is turned round in the jaws. If it is observed
when cutting that the stem is inclined to split further, binding wire should
be applied.

Whether one uses the single, the crossed or the 'Y' support, depends on
the shape of the vase used and the weight of the material. Slender branches
such as long-stemmed carnations require a cross-piece tied to them.
A wooden toothpick may be used for this purpose. This keeps the flower
the right way up when the stem is balanced on the rim of the vase with
its end and cross-piece against the opposite inside of the vase, as shown
in *plates* 20 and 21.

Tulips and narcissi are not easily fixed in *nageire* style arrangements.
Tulips tend to droop, while narcissi and daffodils grow straight up, looking ahead like well-drilled soldiers. Consequently, one cuts tulips fairly
short, and they are placed near the rim of the vase. In modern Japanese
'free-style' arrangements, the petals are sometimes turned gently back
to achieve the effect of a mass of vivid colour. This makes the vase-life
of the blooms even shorter and tends to give an over-blown look; but
it can be effective, giving colour impact to a design exhibited for a short
while. Daffodils respond to gentle stroking near the neck to make them
throw back their heads and look upwards towards the sun. This makes
them more suitable than narcissi for *nageire* arrangements. The many
varieties of narcissi look best in more upright arrangements such as *seika*.
The method of arranging narcissi in *seika* style is dealt with later, as it
is a very precise art.

The eight variations
From the two basic arrangements, *risshin kei* and *keishin kei*, the eight
variations of the Sogetsu School are produced. The stem dimensions and
relative proportions remain unchanged throughout. These variations are
best understood from a study of the accompanying pictures of basic
upright and slanting variations 1 to 5, *moribana* style. The identical variations apply to *nageire*.

Variations 6, 7 and 8 are shown in photographs as they differ completely
from the first five in several respects.

The sixth variation, called the flat or horizontal style, is suitable for
both *moribana* and *nageire* arrangements and may be viewed from four
sides. It is thus very suitable for table centres.

The placements, whether in a low bowl or upstanding in a tall vase,
should divide a circle into three parts. For low bowls, the angles of *shin*,
soe and *hikae* are 85, 75 and 65 degrees respectively. In tall vases, the standard 15, 45 and 75 degrees are used.

The sixth variation in low bowls requires careful filling low down in
the centre to hide the *kenzan*.

The seventh variation is a group of three types of arrangement:
Morimono. Fruit, vegetables, nuts, roots and a few flowers may be used
on a platter, a tray or in a shallow basket. If possible, there should be both

24

25

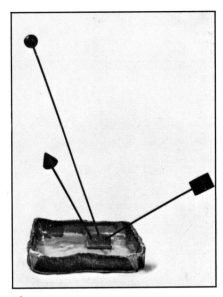

26

27

28

29

30

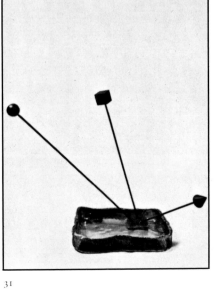

31

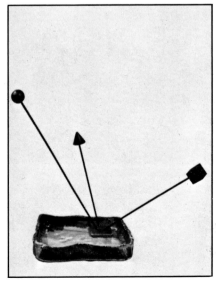

32

33 Slanting style variation 3. *Hikae* comes straight forward at a low angle and *shin* and *soe* are interchanged. The 'fan' behind *hikae* appears to be opening in the opposite direction from that in the upright variation 3.

34 Slanting style variation 4. As in the upright 'omission style', *soe* is omitted. The angle of *shin* is, however, 45° off the vertical instead of 15°. *Hikae* remains at 75°, or more if preferred.

35 Slanting style variation 5. In this style of divided *kenzan* arrangement, *soe* is 15° off the vertical and *shin* is at 45°, again the result of transposition. Water is usually part of the design in *moribana*.

colour harmony and shape contrast. Thus one apple on its side with a second one upright, a colourful leaf and a single bloom can be effective.

Ukibana. Floating flowers are placed in a tray or shallow bowl.

Shikibana. Cut flowers are placed flat, without container or holder, on a table. This spread arrangement also divides a circle in three parts and as it is designed for short period display, in honour of a special guest or for a family celebration, one does not have to consider putting the flowers in water.

37 This *heishin kei* horizontal arrangement reflects full Summer with syringa blossom and deep pink roses in a black chalice container. The lacquer base used here gives balance for the somewhat heavy effect of the flowers.

36 LEFT: This can be viewed from all round and this example is the upright table centre arrangement, Sogetsu variation 6. Three mauve carnations are used for the main stems and two more for *jushis*. The vase is an antique Bohemian glass drinking cup. Fixing technique for the three main stems is by cross pieces cut from the flower stems and tied near the bottom end of the main stems.

38 RIGHT: A tall stoneware vase with brown oxide markings, by Kay Pritchett, shows a *nageire* free style arrangement using pine, driftwood and red roses.

39 LEFT: *Morimono* of black grapes, an orange and bananas with a few violets placed on an olive green Japanese lacquer tray.

41 RIGHT: Combination arrangement, variation 8, using forsythia in variation 1 (*risshin kei*) behind a lower basic *risshin kei*. Dark brown ceramics by Kay Pritchett. Plastic pots are used for a similar arrangement in *plate 46*.

40 LEFT: *Shikibana* of mixed flowers and foliage radiating from a central purple carnation. This is a table centre-piece viewed from all round, and is in honour of a visitor.

The eighth variation is a combination arrangement using two containers, either twin or contrasting tall and low. The arrangements in them should be a pleasing contrast of variation, upright and slanting or hanging, which will be perfectly complementary, each arrangement being complete in its own right.

All basic arrangements are beautiful in their simplicity and are a delightful form of self-expression since the arranger chooses the container, the *oyo* or style, the variation, the flowers and the appropriate means of concealing the mechanics of the arrangement.

Never be dazzled by the sheer beauty and colour of the flowers — they are of secondary importance! It is the structure of the triad of main stems which sets the stage for enhancing a beauty already there. Only when proficiency in simple arrangements is reached may one add the exciting ingredient of imagination to the formula. How wise are they who return repeatedly to the basic arrangements! Only like a dancer limbering up and practising again and again the exercises for ballet, can one reach expertise. The eight variations are perfect for such continuous practice because their variety prevents the student from becoming tired of any one style.

Proficiency comes steadily with constant practice, and we are reminded that Ikebana is also a 'way of life'! Flower arrangement goes hand in hand with the acquisition of self-discipline, patience and tidiness. One becomes a more composed person and there is the deep satisfaction of work well done. But the road is long and our humility is fostered by the knowledge of the innumerable stages ahead. The concept is reflected in the ancient

42 ABOVE: *Morimono* of a yellow apple with black grapes, banana and hellibore flowers in a black lacquered bamboo basket.

43 BELOW: Horizontal style arrangement (*heishin kei*) to be viewed all round. *Shin* and *soe* are pine, *hikae* and *jushis* are double pink tulips. The dish which is used for this arrangement is an Ikaros Rhodian ceramic copied from an antique Turkish plate.

44 ABOVE: *Ukibana*: the flower is supported on hellibore leaves floating in an orange lacquer tray.

45 BELOW: *Ukibana*: floating hellibore flowers with bridging lines of mossy twigs in an olive green lacquer tray.

ritual of *chanoyu*, the tea ceremony. A silvery-toned gong summons the guest, enjoying the garden while he waits, to the tea house. But he must stoop to crawl through the low doorway! Only with humility may he participate in the 'warm stream of sympathy' which unites the host with his guest.

Free style

Free style, or *jiyubana*, should not be attempted until the student's ability has matured with practice and he is able to create his own design by applying imagination to the basic styles and variations. To rush into free style is to court artistic failure, and bars the hope of real progress towards artistry. Only when the *instinct* of balance has been acquired, can one become successful with free style — for which there are no rules. Its

ingredients are originality, movement and balance. It either 'comes off' or it does not. When it fails it is a fiddle-faddle!

Modern trends

Because there are hundreds of schools, each with many styles, Ikebana can never be competitive, nor can it be judged except on the grounds of fine art, the principles of which are universal. Like all art it reflects everyday life and it is perfectly in order that it should follow painting and sculpture. Abstract designs, sculpturally massed colour or texture, and even floral 'mobiles' can be produced. *Objets trouvés* can be used for Ikebana flower arranging as well as for painting, so that all sorts of everyday material such as rope or wire can be employed for their textural and colour qualities.

48 to 54 Stage-by-stage construction of a basic *risshin kei* arrangement using white pear blossom for *shin* and *soe* and pale yellow double tulips for *hikae* and *jushis*. A single megasea leaf serves for *tomi*, hiding the *kenzan* in position 3. The container is a Japanese lavender-coloured ceramic standing on a black lacquer *dai*. The materials and colours evoke thoughts of Spring.

55 LEFT: Scenic style driftwood arrangement on a lacquer base which suggests snowdrops by a lakeside. The flowers are tied in a loose bunch and stand in a *well-kenzan* hidden by moss.

56 to 59 OPPOSITE: Stage-by-stage construction of a basic *risshin kei* using yellow lupin for *shin* and *soe* and a Peace rose for *hikae*. *Jushis* are of lupin and pinks, the *kenzan* being hidden by *tomi* of small stones. Plate 59 shows how the arrangement is improved when an unopened rose with bud attached is used.

Throughout the present decade there has been a trend toward enormous and sculptural exhibition pieces. Foremost in the exploration of this trend is Mr. Sofu Teshigahara, who opened the Sogetsu Art Centre in 1958 and is the Headmaster of Sogetsu Ryu — the 'School of the Grass Moon'. In his arrangements, he uses giant roots and tree trunks as foundations for his beautiful creations. As an internationally famous sculptor, it is natural that he should turn his attention to the exciting media of contorted branches and tangled vines in the search for beautiful shape. Temples, cathedrals, great exhibition halls and the entrances of public buildings call for these enormous displays of artistry. For us there is the abiding joy of creating beautiful arrangements in our homes, and it is interesting to note that there is now a growing popularity for the classical and traditional Ikebana in Japan.

2 What do I need?

Minimum essential equipment

Containers

As far as containers are concerned, the answer to the question 'What have I got at home?' may be found in the kitchen or china cupboard — or possibly in the collection of curios and oddments which we all accumulate over the years.

Do not be deterred by the lack of a special container which looks Japanese. You will certainly find something flat-bottomed and shallow which will hold two or three inches of water. Perhaps that precious sugar basin, the only remaining relic from Grandmother's china tea service, will find a new use at last. Or a plain oven-glass pie dish, a shallow casserole without its lid, or even a roasting pan will serve admirably for practising. Old bottles of unusual shape are useful for *nageire* arrangements. I have an ancient blue Bristol glass cordial bottle, which — being minus its stopper — was bought as a jumble sale for a shilling! Failing such treasures, do not overlook the humble milk bottle. Its identity can be concealed by wrapping with a straw place-mat secured with pins (*plates 61-2*). The dark green glass flagons in which Portuguese wine is sold are very suitable because the coloured glass obscures the stems of material used. In clear glass bottles the stems are visible and therefore distracting. This is undesirable, as it takes away the essential characteristic of an Ikebana container which should usually be 'quiet'. (A quiet container does not pull the eye away from an arrangement. The container is part of the all-over harmony of good design and should enhance the beauty of the foliage and flowers.)

Kenzans or pinholders

Next on our list is a pinholder, this being an item which must be bought. It should be weighty and rustless, and good ones are an investment as they last for years (see *plate 65*).

The Japanese name for a pinholder is *kenzan*, which means 'sword mountain'. It is indeed fascinating, as one progresses, to learn the poetic Chinese and Japanese words which make up the language of Ikebana. For easy reference, the few words in current use are given in a glossary.

Not all schools employ the same holder. The Ohara School favours an open type made of lead and called a *shippo*, meaning 'treasury opening'. The Ikenobo School, as well as certain others, has evolved a simple and patented holder which grips the material in place most effectively. In the West, wire netting and a spongey water-retaining product are aids used in placement techniques. But we shall keep to the Japanese techniques of impaling, wedging and holding up material by using

60 Reconstituted narcissi are arranged in a white porcelain bowl in a *seika* arrangement.

61 and 62 LEFT: Anemones, vitellina willow and yew in an improvised container made from a milk bottle and a straw place-mat. The arrangement is based on *heishin kei* or horizontal style.

63 RIGHT: Sweet William in a two-mouthed container, and used as *hikae* in variation 4 style.

kenzans and the *nageire* fixing technique described in the previous chapter.

Of *kenzans* there are many shapes and sizes devised for various requirements in *moribana* arrangements. Best for the beginner is the *jitsu-getsu* 'sun and moon' type, the main section being circular with a keyed smaller crescent-shaped section which can be joined to the main piece by interlocking. The advantage of this type is that it can be used singly or separately. In the double or '*divided kenzan*' arrangement (variation 5), the two sections are used separately. When using a rather heavy branch which would tend to topple the *kenzan*, the second section can be inverted so that the pins interlock on the first part, making an effective counter-balance. For very weighty and long branches, the large square *kenzans* are best but these sometimes require counter-balance also, particularly for slanting styles. When using an inverted *kenzan*, the uppermost flat bottom of the counter-balance affords a flat surface on which large stones can be placed or on which driftwood can be supported clear of the water.

Hasami or scissors

Thirdly, one requires scissors or clippers. The Japanese ones are called *hasami* and are specially designed for Ikebana. They are obtainable in London at large department stores. Unfortunately, ordinary scissors will not do, but secateurs will serve admirably and, if not already available at home, can be easily obtained at garden stores. The *hasami* are, how-

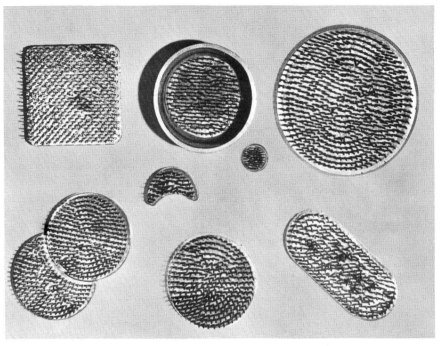

65 RIGHT: Various sizes and types of *kenzan* used for *moribana* arrangements including a *well-kenzan*, the leaden cup of which has pins on the bottom. It is used with basket arrangements and with driftwood on lacquer bases.

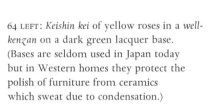

64 LEFT: *Keishin kei* of yellow roses in a *well-kenzan* on a dark green lacquer base. (Bases are seldom used in Japan today but in Western homes they protect the polish of furniture from ceramics which sweat due to condensation.)

ever, easiest to handle and are therefore recommended. They are sturdy enough to cut sharply through a branch up to ½″ thick, or snip the thread-like stem of a violet. For cutting thicker branches, a small saw is necessary. Very attractive, in their brocade cases, are the Japanese tool kits now obtainable in this country. They include scissors, small saw, syringe, chisel and small chopper, together with a tool like an old clock key, for straightening the bent pins of *kenzans*. The syringe is used to spray blooms with mist, which will keep them fresh. It is also used, without its nozzle, to pump water into succulent plant stems. The chisel is used for nicking the sides of stiff branches so that they can be bent into graceful curves — when one becomes more skilful — and the chopper is useful for splitting or cutting thick stems.

It is opportune here to mention the etiquette of flower arranging adopted by all pupils in Japanese schools of floral art. On completion of an arrangement, the table should be absolutely clean. This is part of the required self-discipline, clearing as one goes by placing superfluous and

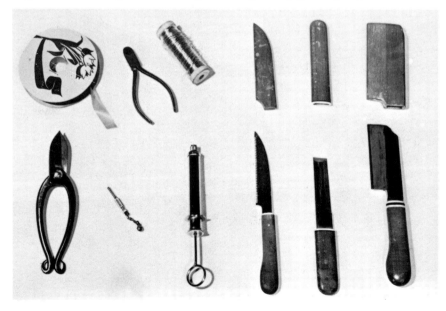

66 The contents of a Japanese Ikebana tool kit, together with gutta percha binding tape, fine binding wire and cutters for wire.

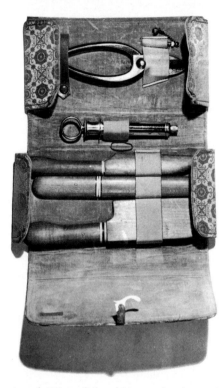

67 and 68 Brocaded tool kit case closed and fastened with its bone toggle, and open showing contents.

69 RIGHT: Upper section of a two-piece celadon glazed container designed by the author and made by Kay Pritchett. This piece serves as a 'compote', as the Japanese call a stemmed bowl, and is used for a late Summer arrangement, as indicated by the full-blown yellow roses, ripe grasses and deep blue hydrangeas.

waste material in a *gomi* — waste tray — beside the arranger. The scissors are then left, handle towards the teacher who comes to inspect the work, at the front of the table. This is the mute and humble tribute to teacher by pupil, implying that the teacher or viewer can do a better arrangement.

Sometimes a teacher, admiring the work, or feeling that the pupil shows marked progress, takes two small pieces of stem from the *gomi* and cuts them to make a small cross, which is silently left beside the arrangement.

With container, *kenzan* and *hasami* you are ready to begin the exploration of one of the most fascinating art forms. These three items will enable you to do many different arrangements in *moribana* style. Your range is doubled, of course, when you do the *nageire* tall vase arrangements and their variations of the basic styles.

Other aids and accessories

Certain technical aids, such as florists' fine wire or 'twistems' — short lengths of wire in greenish paper ribbon — assist the solving of mechanical problems, such as lengthening stems or fixing the cross pieces to hold branches upright in tall vases.

Buckets will also be required. It is better to buy a pair of plastic ones than to suffer the annoyance of requiring a bucket in an emergency — only to find it has flowers or branches in it. So keep two pails ready for using exclusively for your materials. It is obviously better to keep the flowers separate, as the petals can suffer damage all too easily if branches are put in the same bucket.

While one can improvise by using a kettle of cold water — or even a milkbottle — to fill up the container after an arrangement is completed, it is more convenient to buy a water pourer. Plastic ones are inexpensive, but metal stands up to wear and tear rather better.

The above items are the main accessories needed for all but the monumental exhibition pieces. Accessories as understood in Western floral art, are rarely used for Ikebana. Oriental figurines, artefacts and *objets d'art* will not make a flower arrangement a Japanese one!

It is realised that with our shrinking world, due to ever speedier air travel, there is inevitably an exchange of ideas between East and West. Japanese artists come to Europe and America, while we go to Japan in even greater numbers. The Japanese have been quick to observe the techniques of Western floral art and have taken note of the use of selected accessories to underline a mood or often to evoke an idea. It is not surprising, therefore, to find that at least one school — the Chiko — uses what we would broadly term 'accessories' in arrangements with conspicuous success. The Headmaster, Mrs. Kao Naruse, believes that flowers and objects can not only harmonise and balance in colours, size and shape, but that there is an art in bringing out the unity between them. Most frequently used are interesting small dolls, stones and sand. This is but a step further than the other ancient Japanese art of *bonseki* — creating a natural scene in miniature with white sand and stones on a lacquered base or tray. (Mrs. Naruse suggests, for instance, 'A pretty lady, caught in a rain shower'. She notices a lovely flower by the roadside as she hurries along. The doll, portraying a lady in kimono of the Edo period, carries an umbrella, and the rain is suggested by lines drawn in white sand on the lacquer base. The natural foliage and flowers are, of course, in suitable scale.) Such arrangements are ideal for collectors of

70 OPPOSITE: Modern upright arrangement in an antique dark blue bottle interpreting the theme 'Spectre de la rose'. Bleached wistaria vine makes the design with a single red rose.

objets d'art who seek an interesting way to display their collection.

Even more interesting is the fact that certain classical arrangements did actually use accessories in a restrained manner, despite the emphatic 'No', given by the great Masters in reply to the question, 'Is it in order to use accessories in Ikebana?'. They are naturally, and rightly, afraid that indiscriminate use would soon reduce a fine art to an arty-crafty affair. It should be mentioned, so that the student of Ikebana knows where he stands, that — according to Flower Master Norman J. Sparnon who studied at the Ikenobo and Sogetsu Schools in Japan — sixteenth century scrolls depicted a vase of flowers with an incense burner, a candlestick and the implements for handling the incense. The accessories mentioned were temple offerings made with the flowers. When the *tokonoma* became a feature of Japanese homes, for the display of scroll and Ikebana, a tall table was introduced and the incense burner was placed on the top shelf, with the Ikebana on the lower shelf. It may be that the purpose of the incense was a dual one — to symbolise religious devotion and to dispel small flying insects. We have all seen the efficacious spirals and sticks of incense sold all over the Orient for burning to repel mosquitoes.

As your acquisition of knowledge and skill in arranging grows, so will your collection of useful items. It is as well to start collecting screw-cap glass jars to contain various grades of pebbles and small stones, sand and small sundries. Ikebana has a wider world to show you, for on your rambles and holidays your eye becomes more alert and roves so that you observe much that you never noticed before. Seek beauty in commonplace things. Trees, bared of leaves in winter, reveal their characteristic lines — which are all different. Previously they were just trees, but now they are seen lifting their bare arms heavenward. Even when branches are naturally downward-sloping, their tips are often turned up toward the life-giving sun. Every bud or leaf-shoot reveals the principle of 'enfolding space'. These lines, when used for Ikebana, enliven the design with flowing and gentle curves. Certain plant material shows qualities of line hitherto unperceived — slender curves, irregular angles and hanging growth — all affecting the mood of a design.

Do not curb your self-expression. Let line, texture and colour suggest beautiful or fantastic form and movement.

3 What shall I use?

71 A mobile of plaited date palm camels and dried calyxes of desert flowers. Sheep bells are added to complete a pastoral as well as an audio-kinetic effect. Gold sequins are used for the eyes as they have a brilliant reflecting property which gives an almost third dimensional effect.

72 RIGHT: This abstract arrangement shows how contrast is achieved. Dried grasses soar outwards, while a single red rose is contained within the fish trap.

Materials and design

This question confronted me in an alarming way when I was touring Tunisia and arrived at my hotel, on the island of Djerba, where I was to give a demonstration. This was arranged for the following day as I expected to be tired after the long desert drive from the oasis of Gabes from which I had brought flowers in pails of water. I hastened to have these put in a cool dark place, and the manager proposed his air-conditioned apartment. He also announced an unexpected treat. Tunisia's two most beautiful dancing girls had arrived and would entertain us after dinner that night.

Djerba is thought to be the desert island of the Lotophagi, Homer's lotuseaters, where Ulysees' crew were so dilatory in returning to their ship after shore-leave, due to the properties of the strange fruit. The white sands, the palm trees and dark blue sea are incredibly beautiful, so that a bathe, drink and dinner were a delightful prelude to the coming appearance of the Arab dancers.

Soon the throbbing drums and a plaintive flute announced their entry as they seemed to float down the marble staircase to the courtyard. They looked so graceful and they carried on their heads baskets *filled with my flowers*! I am told that my face was very red for I guessed that they had changed in the manager's apartment and found my flowers completely irresistible.

I composed myself quickly, for they looked so lovely quivering with extraordinary suppleness and grace in their silk robes, their golden anklets tinkling as their bare feet moved over the marble floor. I just hoped that they would replace my flowers carefully in the pails of water. Alas! At the end of the performance the baskets were emptied as all the blooms were tossed to the applauding audience!

'What shall I use indeed?' I thought, 'well, for a start, my head'. I had less than twenty-four hours to plan how to use aloes, date palms fantastic coral stones riddled with holes, and perhaps I could find one date palm with an opening sheath of cream blossom. In the hotel garden there were oleanders without flowers but last year's seed-pods were of interesting form, like tawny and crescent-shaped boats. I had also found and brought with me from Carthage, where I had been prior to my visit to Djerba, some contorted rosemary roots.

I recall my Japanese teacher once saying that in modern arrangement it need not necessarily be flowers to be Ikebana. The Sogetsu School teaches that all materials can be used to create beautiful form. The Ikenobo School — the oldest and most traditional in Japan — has combined peacock feathers with entwining gilded branches in a monumental *rikka*. This symbolised the male and female elements in a ceremonial composition designed for the wedding of Flower Master Senei Ikenobo.

73 Variation 5. An arrangement of iris illustrating the effect of combining vertical and horizontal lines. Black and turquoise ceramic made by the author.

74 The oblique lines of dried grass might suggest the sun's rays lighting the corner of a garden in summer where there are yellow roses near blue hydrangeas.

The lower half of a celadon jar designed by the author and thrown by Kay Pritchett. The top half is shown in *plate 69*, and the whole vase in *plate 82*.

You can use anything you please providing you leaven it with imagination. Skill and practice will enable you to create beautiful form, but it must be remembered that the imagination must not run riot.

On the occasion when my flowers disappeared I had watched my guide passing the time making plaited camels out of palm fronds. I persuaded him to plait several for me in different sizes and together we set about constructing a mobile. It was fun because as the camels were suspended they seemed to come to life and started rotating in the light breeze.

Since the three basic requirements of Ikebana are design, depth and colour, one must consider the characteristics of line to be able to design. Paul Klee once said, describing a squiggly line doodled at random, 'It is just a line going for a walk'. He meant, of course, a line having the quality of movement.

Line characteristics of materials
Vertical lines, especially when standing on a horizontal line, are devoid of any suggestion of movement. They give the idea of strength, tran-

75 *Suishin kei* of mimosa and driftwood in a cylindrical vase by Kay Pritchett. Modern Japanese arrangements often use driftwood.

76 Modern two-mouthed container, designed by the author and made by Kay Pritchett, used for *suishin kei* of Sweet William and clematis leaves. The dark hardwood base of Argentine algaroba gives weight to the slender vase base.

quillity and stability. Plant growth having this characteristic includes bamboo, bulrushes, chrysanthemums, pholx, gladioli, iris, lilies, narcissi, pampas, reeds, tulips and wheat. All upright-growing material looks best in low, shallow bowls.

Slanting and oblique lines suggest movement, and curved lines have a grace essentially feminine and rhythmic. Slanting plant growth includes azaleas, hydrangeas, magnolia, pine, prunus, maple and quince. Such plants can be arranged in both low and tall containers.

The curves of spiral lines have pronounced rhythm and suggest the cyclic pattern of the seasons; equally they convey the hope that someone going on a journey may return soon. Hence spirals are used in arrangements to wish anyone a good journey and quick return. Sometimes a loose knot of weeping willow, either in bud or stripped of leaves, is used for this. It is interesting that the spiral was a decorative form of line as early as the second millennium B.C., and it is thought by archaeologists to have represented eternity.

Material which grows hanging is very popular for Ikebana. It includes asparagus fern, briony or bitter-sweet, clematis, eucalyptus, forsythia,

spirea or bridal-wreath and morning glory. Any of these may be used
in a hanging arrangement, such as a crescent moon suspended, or a
gourd on a wall tablet. Hanging arrangements also look well in tall
vases. The Ohara School calls this 'cascade style'.

The angular lines of certain plant material suggest quite forcibly rest-
lessness, sharpness and even cruelty. Such material can be used effectively to express a mood of anxiety or frustration. It is a curious fact
that the creation of such an arrangement has the almost miraculous
effect of inspiring hope and confidence.

Enclosing shapes

In the analysis of characteristics affecting choice of material we have so
far only considered line. We must also consider the shape of an arrangement. All schools have embodied the main artistic principles, based
on line, in their methods of teaching, but the Ichiyo School stresses the
value of giving great attention to the shape *enclosing* the lines. Round-
ness, for instance, suggests smoothness and age-worn effects. One is reminded of the stones from river beds which are rounded and almost
polished. Oval shape is considered suggestive of uneven planes and in-
stability. It thus conforms with certain moods of nature evoking the
idea of fleeting beauty. On the other hand, an oblong or rectangular
shape suggests the quietness and persistence of stable things. Square
shapes give an impression of weight, and so of immobility. They are seldom
used in Ikebana unless to emphasize mood. A square-shaped arrangement of close-growing and bare branches of blackthorn imprisoning a
few stems of upright narcissi might, for example, be used to express

a theme of 'courage in adversity', or 'beauty triumphant'. Triangular shape immediately conjures up the idea of defined boundaries to the variations it encloses. This shape is particularly beautiful when it is a scalene triangle having no two angles alike. As an outline of shape, containing even the simplest basic design, it leads to the surprising discovery that good designs in Ikebana can usually be enclosed within an imaginary scalene triangle, and this in turn affects choice of material.

The Japanese are particularly fond of the bleached branches of edgeworthia, which they call *mitsumata*. The branches of this shrub sprout in threes from the parent stem. When the branches are placed upside down, the succession of triple lines suggests the stark and cold stability of monumental forms. One recalls Gothic arches or Egyptian obelisks. Used obliquely, *mitsumata* has the movement of lightning, while placed horizontally it creates an impression of calmness and permanence.

Sculptural forms

From shapes, we proceed to sculptural considerations. Our modern sculptors use an element which the Chinese discovered and which the Japanese have always found significant in good design. I refer to the void — space or nothingness, a shape suggested by an incomplete line or even a mere hole in a mass. The void is the presentation of something omitted, and leaves the imagination to complete the picture. An example is the Sogetsu fourth variation — the style of omission — which omits *soe* and has only *shin* and *hikae*.

Void is particularly attractive when it is a waterworn hole in a stone or rock. The Japanese treasure stones which have been found on their wanderings on the mountainside, or by the shore. This appreciation of lovely stone shapes has always been instinctive. In a beautifully landscaped Japanese garden, however small, one often finds Mount Sumera, the sacred Buddhist mountain, represented by a large pointed stone surrounded by seven smaller ones. Stones are used extensively in Ikebana. Pebbles hide the *kenzan* or suggest the 'fish-path' in a pool where water plants grow. Beautifully worn stones have been handed down through generations as heirlooms. Some are exquisitely mounted on carved and polished stands. Others are displayed in a bed of sand gravel in low bowls. Interesting shapes of rough stone are sometimes used in *bonzai*, the roots of the dwarf tree worming over the mossy stone to reach the potted earth. This love of beautiful stones derives from earliest times, when people considered these things as nature spirits to be worshipped, since they were manifestations of *kami*, a god.

The use of stones (plates 91-95)

The precious water-worn stones are called *sui seki* and are not easily come by, usually being found in dried-up river beds, where centuries of mountain torrents from melting snows or heavy rains have polished them. We are content, however, to find a knobbly flint in a newly ploughed field, or smooth stones piled up on a pebble beach. Even if our search for stones has a negligible yield, we can always use clinker, which, painted matt white, simulates coral very well. This, however, is a fast disappearing material as gas or oil replaces solid fuel.

Never despise stones as a substitute for flowers in an interpretation of the Ikebana triad of *shin*, *soe* and *hikae*. A typical stone arrangement would be a tall and pointed stone with a medium sized one alongside it in a tray. A third and smaller stone would balance these on the other

80 RIGHT: The sharpness and angular lines of the thorn, the flame coloured double tulips and the exotic seed pod in a Chinese blue jar demonstrate how cruelty can be suggested.

81 Interlocked and oblique lines of bleached driftwood recall the relentless evanescence of beauty. Yet another bud will unfold afterwards.

82 A cascade or *suishin kei* arrangement
in a tall celadon vase which uses both
sections of the two-piece container designed
by the author for using a *kenzan* as in
the chalice-type containers.

side. Sand sprinkled and raked with a small *kenzan* would suggest water
swirling round the stones. Balance would be achieved by making the
sweep of water more pronounced round the smaller stone. This is a
miniature of the austere rock gardens of temples in Japan. The seashore can be suggested by a few shells and small water plant flowers
or reeds placed discreetly. The art lies in leaving out everything that
does not help to suggest the chosen theme. In the West, we habitually
pile in everything which is to hand. Lamentably some Japanese Schools

83 ABOVE: This *nageire* arrangement shows the linear design, and for *jushis* pink and deep rose carnations are placed near the rim of the vase.

84 ABOVE RIGHT: A *chabana* arrangement of pink camellias in a Japanese style modern ceramic, designed by the author and made by Kay Pritchett. There is a suggestion of calligraphy in the glazing.

are so obsessed with Westernisation that they copy our faults too. One wonders who is swallowing whom; or whether a 'universal style' of flower arranging will emerge. Probably the West will be custodian of the classic and traditional styles until Japan has passed through the free-style phase and until the banality of the hybrid 'linear' or 'oriental style' arrangements makes them outmoded. Western floral art is exquisite in the hands of the true floral artist, and the influence of Ikebana has brought about poor imitations which bewilder the public. Let it be widely known by all organisers of Flower Shows that Ikebana is not competitive, nor can it be assessed except by a teacher of one of the twenty-odd accredited schools followed by the exhibitor. Happily there is a growing list of such qualified teachers throughout the world, particularly in the United States, and Australia has its own Flower Master in the person of Norman J. Sparnon — the first European man to gain recognition in the art.

While discussing the subject of design and composition, mention must be made of an essentially Japanese quality *shibui*, or 'refined poverty'. This implies beauty created from the most commonplace things yet remaining naturalistic and charming in a simple way.

Finally there is the consideration of the ancient concept derived from Chinese philosophy and known as the principle of *yin* and *yang*, having the significance of darkness and brightness respectively. In Japan the

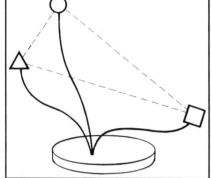

85 A triangular shape gives the impression of defined boundaries, and is particularly beautiful when it is a scalene triangle.

86 The rectangular shape of the container with angular texturing suggests stability. Montbretia is used for *shin* and its supporting stem and also for *soe*, while berberis is used for *hikae*.

56

terms have become *in* and *yo* but they have the same meaning, and represent the harmony of perfect complementary contrasts when balanced. *In* is the female element and is negative, passive or receiving. *Yo* is positive, erect and is the active male element. While *in* is dark, *yo* is bright. Harmony only comes when the balance is perfect. The principle applies equally to colours and therefore affects one's choice of flowers when the arrangement is to be traditional or classic. The colours for *yo* are the reds, rosy hues and purple. Those for *in* are blues, yellows and white. There are innumerable pairs of complements in this positive and negative order — sun and moon, left and right, heaven and earth, good and evil, and so on. An important pair to remember is the part of the plant growth looking towards the sun: *yo* is the front or positive side, while that looking toward the earth, *in*, is the back or negative element. All floral art having originated with the *rikka*, one would ex-

87 A dry material winter arrangement of bleached fern, lotus seed pods and twisted vines forming leaf-like shapes. All material suggests the past. The deep blue Japanese ceramic bowl gives a colour note to the neutral tones of the dried material.

88 LEFT: Double arrangement of white iris. As the driftwood 'bridge' gives weight to the base, *shin* has a supporting stem and *hikae* likewise in the right hand group. Hydrangea leaves hide the *kenzan* and the view of water in the dark blue ceramic *suiban* is attractive. It should be noted, however, that this is not the type of iris used in Japan; these leaves having a less imposing shape have been cut to a point below the blooms.

89 RIGHT: The tangled lines of dried palmetto inflorescence with red tulips arranged in *nageire* style, using a chalice-type vase, convey thoughts of frustration and harshness overcome by the contemplation of beautiful flowers.

90 OPPOSITE BELOW: This simple *chabana*, or tea ceremony arrangement for hanging as a wall arrangement would also be called a *kakebana*. A honey-coloured and waisted gourd with attractive surface markings has clivia with vitellina willow with which the bronze leaves of berberis harmonise perfectly.

pect to find the principle employed in these arrangements, which have perfect balance.

It is as well to know of these concepts although they need not concern the beginner except when viewing the arrangements of the experts at exhibitions as, without this knowledge, the arrangements would not be understood. The beginner should, however, consider most carefully the matter of balance if a good design is to be produced. This exposition partly explains the Japanese saying that 'the flowers will tell one the way to arrange them'. The type of material will also dictate the type of container required to achieve the perfect balance. This principle is the origin of all that is taught today and applied to Western floral art. That is why the Japanese admire our style of arranging — except when they get a sort of 'accessories indigestion'.

The question 'What shall I use?' is not a new one. In the sixteenth century Hideyoshi — Japan's military genius — was once in camp at Odawara and he craved the solace of flowers in his tent. The Tea Master Rikyu, who always accompanied him on his campaigns, having nothing to create Ikebana, used a horse's bit to fix a few wild flowers in a shallow

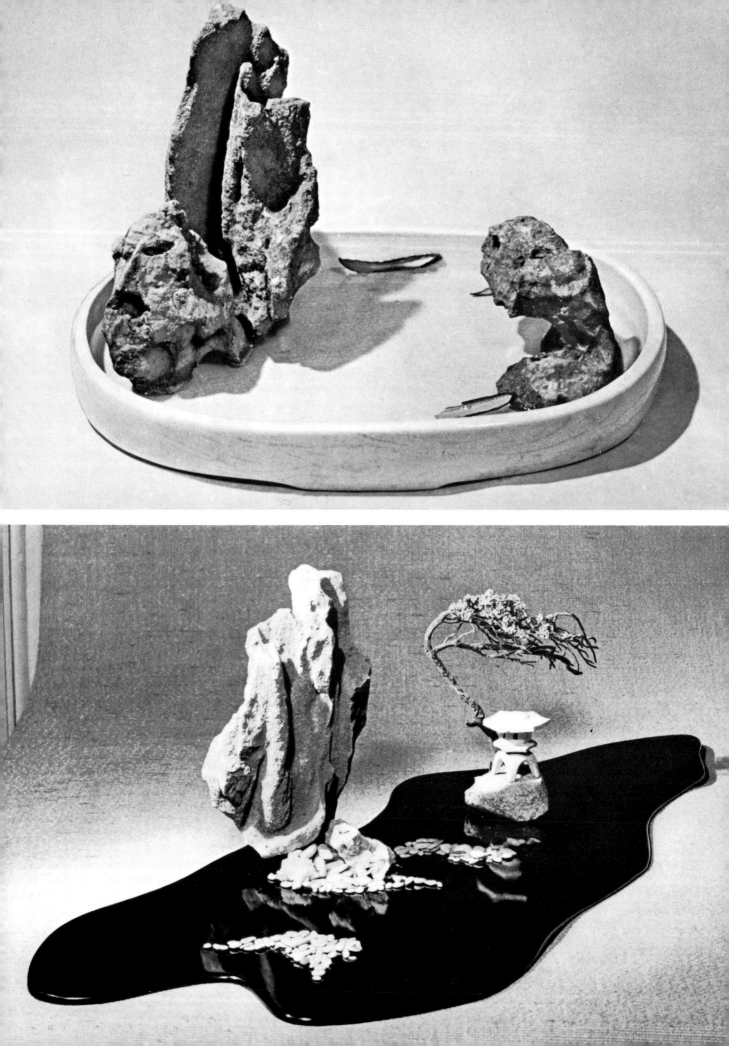

91 LEFT: A scenic arrangement of water-worn stones having interesting shapes are placed in an old Japanese *suiban*. The illusion of mountains and lake is created by floating the husks of oleander seed pods on the water to suggest fishermen's boats thus giving 'scale'.

92 LEFT: Stones and pebbles on a black lacquer base, resembling a pool, create the effect of a Japanese stone garden, scale being created by a miniature stone lantern and a mossy twig suggesting a wind-swept tree.

93 RIGHT: An interesting water-worn hole in this stone, a mass of bunched campanulas and feathery wild flowers recall the mountains of Crête in this free style arrangement which is based on basic *risshin kei* using the stone as *hikae*.

tub, which was set on a wooden slab with an attractive stone beside it. Hideyoshi was so impressed that on another occasion he asked Rikyu to send his daughter to the palace that he might test her skill in the difficult task of arranging a branch of peace blossom without a holder. She pondered a while, and then plucked some blossom and floated it on the surface of the water. Thus was the style *ukibana*, or floating flowers, created.

The favoured branches
If you have a garden, you will soon grow shrubs and special flowers for

94 LEFT: In a small terra cotta ceramic, made by the author to suggest a water-worn stone, hedgerow grasses and buttercups make a simple but pleasing design to illustrate *shibui*, the charm of refinement in simplicity.

95 RIGHT: Another illustration of *shibui*, the movement of pale grasses suggesting splashing water.

Ikebana. Remember that some of the humblest plants are chosen for their various qualities in arranging. Reed is favoured because of its straight and fine upright lines. You will probably learn to leave laurel alone, except the less usual variety known as 'Portuguese laurel' which is more attractive than the symmetrical leaves of common laurel. Rhododendron, with its pretty groups of leaves growing radially, also has stems of great variety and often lovely curves when it has had to seek the sunlight from the shady underside of the bush. It is the ideal branch material for beginners to practice all styles. In contrast, the common hawthorn is, as a general rule, angular, bushy and spiky, but this too can be found

with interesting and long branches having good lines. The stunted bushy parts can be used imaginatively for modern arrangements.

Holly, stark green or variegated, is prickly to handle but makes very attractive arrangements for Christmas. It looks lovely with driftwood. Even the great Flower Masters of Japan have been induced to create designs to set off the dark green leaves with contrasting baubles and tinsel. And why not candles? They are surely a permissible accessory today if they were so with the incense burner in traditional arrangements.

Oak is a favourite branch for all seasons. In Spring the leaves are small and attractively vivid green; it is also a good bender. Beech is lovely in Spring; and for Autumn, maples or mountain ash are favoured.

Weeping willow is a firm favourite, and lends itself admirably to being incorporated with pine in monumental exhibition arrangements. There are several varieties of willow and the *vitellina* 'egg-yolk' stems on pollarded trees, which I found in Normandy, had an especial appeal, their orange-yellow shoots being like sunbursts in the early morning light.

The alder has strong angular and straight-line characteristics, suggestive of restless or unstable mood when it is used without leaves to show the lines. The yew, especially the variety known as Irish yew, is popular and a good bender. It is a most suitable greenery for traditional arrangements such as the classic Koryu School *honde ike* arrangement.

Flowering currant is one of my favourites for Spring arrangements. The blossom does not drop, and it grows abundantly and hardily. It has graceful curves and looks pretty with pink tulips or hyacinths.

Whole books have been written about the camellia and innumerable hybrids have been produced. The subject is worthy of study, but a few remarks must suffice here. Japan has always had its camellias as England has had its roses. An old scroll of the seventeenth century shows how the cherished camellias were used for Ikebana: in a basket, a single bloom in a bowl and in a hanging arrangement; a spray of camellia in a hanging arrangement would sometimes be used for the Tea Ceremony. While we can substitute our various roses for camellias in arrangements, the two flowers are quite disparate in most arrangements. The strange fact is that the rose has quite captivated the Orient and in the same way the West has 'discovered' the camellia, which for nearly two centuries has been an exotic bloom to us.

In Japan some three hundred varieties flourish, one-third of these being wild mountain varieties which yield edible oil-producing nuts. The nuts are also selected for shape and size, polished and carved into beautiful designs. The Japanese are inately representative artists of impeccable taste and great talent, inspired by animals, birds and insects, as well as flora. I have two such nuts carved as crabs, which I believe are carved from camellia nuts. The work is as fine as that of any ivory *netsuke*, as they are tiny boxes (see *plate 102*).

When camellia is used for Spring Ikebana, the branches are not primarily for the display of line. Instead, the most is made of the glossy green leaves as a setting for the flowers and partially hidden buds. Although camellias are very successfully grown in Europe in the suitable type of soil, (there is a vast nursery exclusively for camellias at Egham, near London), one does not, unfortunately, often find branches with buds intact in florists' shops. Doubtless this is because the flowers tend to fall easily and do not stand up to transport. The *samurai* (knights) of former ages regarded any fallen blossoms as an ill omen, and therefore rarely used either camellias or cherry blossom for Ikebana.

We esteem our roses when the bud is unfurling, but the Japanese like to see the yellow tuft of pistils on the opened camellias, and they favour single-petalled flowers with large pistils. Mr Tohko Adachi, a great Flower Master and founder of his school, is also an expert on camellias. He has been quoted as saying: 'As in man, the heart is more important than the flesh'.

The European and American developments of various species have surprised Japan, whose experiments seem to have been confined to *bonzai* dwarf tree propagation, the highly specialised technique and secrets of which were always closely guarded. Over three thousand varieties of camellia have been developed overseas from the original wild *yuki tsubaki*. I recall on a recent visit to Florida, I was given the freedom of my host's garden which was surrounded by magnificent varieties of camellia of many hues and sizes. It seemed rather dreamlike to be able to cut branch after branch of crimson flowers for an Ikebana in a white bowl — the traditional colours of crimson and white being those used for a 'happy occasion' in Japan.

97 LEFT: Free style arrangement illustrating geometric forms which can be made with reed. Short chalice-shaped vase in celadon glaze by Kay Pritchett.

98 A Christmas arrangement of holly and baubles in the upright style of omission, variation 4, where *soe* is left out. This has the required depth and colour for modern Ibekana.

99 Christmas arrangement in basic slanting style. The baubles are optional as there is colour in the red berries used for *tomi* and there is a metallic glitter in the stone of crystaline ore assisting the berries conceal the *kenzan*. In Japan the colours red and white denote a 'happy occasion', but golden baubles would look pretty with tawny chrysanthemums.

I think, however, that camellias look their best floating in the stone basins which collect spring-water in the typical tea house gardens of Japan. The lichen-covered rock basin, the refreshing sound of falling water coming from the bamboo chute and one or two floating blossoms are perfectly in keeping with the simplicity of the Tea Ceremony. The camellia, after all, symbolises contentment.

Reeds, flags and bulrushes are invaluable material for Ikebana, both modern and free-style. New Zealand flax is also popular, and has the same severe tapering lines as sanseveria but is more flexible. This permits it to be bent into loops, curls, or used where straight lines are required.

The wistaria vine has always enraptured the Japanese. There is even an elegantly stylised dance called *fujimusme*, or wistaria maiden, which was introduced by a famous *kabuki* actor and is now very popular with young girls. The vines bend to make spirals very easily, like large tendrils. Grape tendrils being too small for visual impact, the idea is con-

100 LEFT: A Christmas arrangement subtly suggesting the Nativity. A mass of pure white chrysanthemums in a 'blanc de chine' white bowl with enduring pine symbolises the mother while a single gold-hued flower with a gilded vine halo represents the Child. A Mexican straw angel behind trumpets the 'Glad Tidings'.

101 RIGHT: A classical *seika* arrangement in Koryu School *honde ike* style uses oak for *shin, shinmae, nagashi* and *uke* branches. Small yellow chrysanthemums are used for the *tome* stem which comes between *uke* and *shin* – like flowers in a valley – in this five-branch arrangement. The container is an antique *usubata* with damascened pattern of birds in flight and it stands on a *kwadai*.

veyed by simulated tendrils made of wistaria vine. Twisted and tangled trunk stems also suggest the persistent force of growth and the seeking of the sun's life-giving rays.

Chestnut branches are popular and the green burrs are often used instead of flowers for 'fill-in' purposes. Viburnam is also a most useful shrub at all seasons, as is pyrocanthus, both having attractive autumn berries, and being especially suited for hanging arrangements.

Nor must we overlook the prime favourites for bending. These are broom, pussy-willow and willow tortuosa. When dealing with pussy-willow great care is necessary to avoid knocking off the silvery catkins. As it is invariably bent to give a curve, its easy-bending property endears it to all arrangers. The tortuosa variety has also won admirers on all sides because of its flowing lines, which suggest rippling water.

These are just a few of the possible tree and shrub materials that can be used. As from a long list of acquaintances one inevitably selects close

102 A pair of identical carved nuts in the form of small boxes. These are thought to be camellia nuts. On one side a crab is depicted, the base having a fish and lobster.

friends, so too one soon has favourites in the plant world.

Should you be without a garden you will not have the same facilities as those who enjoy these amenities or live in the country near hedges, fields and woodland. You will, however, no doubt have good friends who, knowing your difficulty, will certainly give you prunings and cuttings. It is observed that, with the ever-growing popularity of flower arranging, florists are now co-operating by carrying stocks of foliage, branches and even flowers in the bud — especially daffodils and narcissi. How different, and so much more natural, are arrangements done with flowers placed while in bud! And there is the added pleasure of watching them as they unfold each day.

Dried materials serve their purpose in winter, when Ikebana made with fresh flowers would be short-lived in any room that is cosily warm. It is also the expensive time of year for all flowers. A seasonal arrangement of dried material, suggesting the country in winter, can be very beautiful and last for a long time. It is wise to gather and dry material for this purpose in summer, storing it hanging upside down, or in boxes, for winter use.

There is on the market much painted and dyed dry material. Unless the colouring is applied with severe restraint, it seems to offend good taste. The natural russet, beige and brown tones of dried material have a charm of their own. Seed pods are especially lovely, and some even suggest the Regency panels of Grinling Gibbons in wood carving — as long as they have harmonising colours suggestive of wood. They can, of course, be spray-gilded with effect for Christmas decoration.

If colour is imperative, to give a cheerful note on grey days, a brightly coloured container will be useful, or two or three bright flowers may be added as a focal note. One of my own favourites for dried materials is a deep rose Chinese bowl having an incised design under the glaze. It gives colour and life to dried materials ranging from pale beige to deep mahogany.

The techniques of cutting and bending (plate 108)
As in painting, it is better to stand than to sit, when arranging flowers. Formerly the Japanese used the sitting-kneeling posture, but now it is the practice to take a stance the same distance from the bench or table as the arrangement is behind the edge of the working space. Then without moving the firmly planted feet — one of which should be forward — one can lean back the better to view the work. This stance also lends force both to bending and cutting.

Some teachers instruct pupils to cut downwards with the tip of a branch towards the floor. Others favour cutting upwards. But I prefer the latter method, as one can inspect a branch carefully, twisting it to the angle it will have toward the viewer when placed. It should be held with the tip uppermost and the bow of the curve outwards toward the left. Then, if the cut is fairly vertical at the bottom end, a nice sharp wedge will result, the point of which is on the longer side of the stem.

The same angle of wedge is applied if a branch, because of its thickness, has to be cut by a saw. After cutting, it is as well to make a slit up the centre of the stem to aid water-rising. I find it easy to saw thick branches if one rests the branch flat on a *kenzan*, so that the pins grip it firmly and prevent it from slipping about. With a pad of folded paper under the left hand one can safely apply pressure on branch and *kenzan*, and the sawing is quickly completed at the desired angle.

103 OPPOSITE: An example of variation 5 using bulrushes with a few water-side wild flowers. Megasea leaves are used as *tomi*, effectively hiding the *kenzan*. The material itself effects the suggested bridging between the *shin* and *soe* group on the right and the *hikae* group on the left.

104 BELOW LEFT: An example of imagination applied to an arrangement of reeds and mauve chrysanthemums in a *well-kenzan*. The fan, through which all the stems pass, serves to hide the *kenzan*.

105 BELOW RIGHT: Pussy-willow *shin* and *soe* with supporters are bent to good curved lines, while *hikae*, a short stem of the same material, shows its catkins in the 'window' aperture of this *niju kiri* double container of Ikenobo School style. In the top part window iris echo the *shin* line of the lower grouping.

Sometimes a branch is too thick and weighty to stand up in a *kenzan*. It is then necessary to screw the branch to a slab of wood about half an inch thick and roughly the size of a large envelope. One or two *kenzans* placed on such a foot will keep the balance firmly. *Kenzan* and foot are, of course, concealed finally with stones or other *tomi*, such as large leaves. (Hosta and magasea are suitable as *tomi*, being in scale for large arrangements.)

The slant of such a large branch will determine the angle of the cut, the surface of which must rest flat on the slab of wood. It is best to gauge this angle carefully and to mark the branch with a clearly defined line as a guide for the saw-cut. I recommend the use of a brass countersunk headed screw for fixing as it will not rust (and so discolour the water); neither will it protrude from the underside of the wood, causing it to wobble, instead of resting flat in the bowl. For very large arrangements there are available metal branch-clamps, anchored to a weighty flat stone. Whatever method is used it should be recalled that a branch also

72

106 *Suishin kei* used in a grey chalice-type
ceramic with willow (salix tortuosa)
and pink double tulips.

requires water and the outer surface should be peeled of bark and sliced
with a few radial slits to permit water-rising.

Branches often have to be bent to produce the attractive bow-like
curve required for good Ikebana. Unless one has an unlimited supply
of branches, bending is essential, and the simple technique must be
mastered as one of the first steps toward competence. For the beginner,
there are two facts to be borne in mind. The first is that if a branch is
not green, due to sap in it, the branch will snap. The second is that bending should never be attempted at joints or nodes, as they are called.
The bending should be slow and accompanied by a twisting motion
exerted with the right hand. This twisting stretches the peripheral fibres
and makes bending easier. As when cutting, a firm stance is necessary
and in this case it is well to press the left elbow against the side to improve the grip of the left hand on the branch. Both hands should hold
the branch by placing the thumb tips together on the underside and
then gripping with all four fingers of both hands. In this way the bending

107 A modern *seika*-style arrangement of glossy brown seed pods, dried grasses, bleached fern and dried flowers in a deep rose Chinese bowl. The *kenzan* is hidden by small pebbles.

108 RIGHT: Notches and wedges for bending.

takes place over the thumb-balls which are cushion-like. Patience is naturally required.

In traditional and classical arrangements the bow curvature of main lines was of such great importance for good design that several shallow notches were made on one side of the branch, at points where bending was to take place. Thick branches obviously required larger notches, and small wedges were often forced into the cut to hold the bend. Normally the most satisfactory notch is one made at a sharp angle rather than at right angles to the side of the stem. I think, however, it is practical to leave notching until one is fairly expert and to make the best of natural curves, as found on tree and shrub material. This also has the advantage of speeding up the eye-training for selective purposes.

Finally there is the hot water immersion process. This is particularly suited to wistaria vines. Often it is necessary to set a bend by tying a loop which has been bent and then putting it in cold water for a few hours. Green vines can be set by tying and leaving to dry in a box for a few weeks.

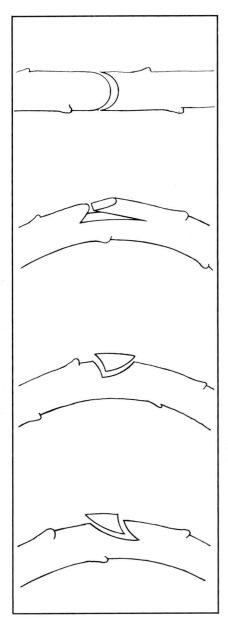

Pussy-willow is the best bender of all, and a practical way to overcome the loss of catkins from breaking off is to wrap the bunch of stems in a towel or newspaper for the entire length. It is then possible to twist and bend the tightly wrapped parcel, tying down the loop and putting the stems in water to set, if necessary. Inevitably some buds are broken, but the loss is minimised.

Broom is also bent in this way but with a less twisting motion as it is inclined to spiral easily. The beginner should practise with broom and pussy-willow, as these are the easiest materials to manipulate.

Grasses and reeds are not bent as a rule unless in the mass like broom or for modern arrangements. They are usually bound together about two inches from the bottom of the bundle, normally with thin wire or raffia, and fairly tightly. The bunch is then cut at a position half an inch below the binding. Holding this cut flush in the palm of the hand a circular motion is imparted to the bundle while pressing it against the palm. This makes the reeds splay out attractively like a sunburst.

The seasonal character of arrangements

Today Ikebana reflects not only the season but also everyday life. Since 1930 this ancient art has developed towards an extraordinary freedom of expression in Japan where the Westernizing process has become almost an obsession. It is quite in order to use any material of interesting shape, colour or texture, preferably 'out of context' one might say. Plant material is used living or dead. Aspidestra leaves are utilised, with banana tatters, bleached or painted black for dramatic effect. The object is to use *form* and lose identity. It can lead to disaster, and indeed it once did, when I used copper pot scourers as the corollas of fantastic flowers. Unfortunately the scourers are too familiar to us all to lose their identity easily, their power of suggestion evoking only memories of unpleasant chores. Some of my colleagues at the teachers' exhibition thought my 'joke' distasteful, sniffed audibly and passed on!

Ikebana can, however, be done without flowers, using tree stumps, roots and wires bent and tangled into form. Even lathe metal turnings have been used as they have an attractive spiral form, shining like shimmering corkscrews. It is only natural to explore the gimmicks — for which the Japanese will doubtless invent a word! The golden rule is nothing in excess and no exhibitionism.

There is difficulty nowadays in keeping strictly to seasonal arrangements, as flowers are flown all over the world. The seasonal characteristic of good Ikebana is thus too easily lost. We know, however, that beautiful as the colour harmony might be, a mixture of autumn-tinted berries with spring flowers looks wrong.

Nearly every country has a national flower emblem. The chrysanthemum is associated with Japan, the sixteen-petal variety being for the exclusive use of the Emperor. Cherry blossom is also recognised as the national flower. Then there is a flower for each lunar month of the year. And with each flower or plant there is the charming symbolism of tradition. Doing an Ikebana for some auspicious occasion in Japan would demand much careful thought and a vast knowledge of plant lore.

The floral calendar of the East comprises pine, plum and peach for the first three months, cherry for April, iris and peony for May and June. July is the month for morning glory and August is lotus month. For September there is a simple bouquet of wild flowers known as 'the seven plants of autumn' and called in Japanese *aki no nanasaka*. This was

75

mentioned in an eighth century poem, and has appeared in paintings throughout the centuries. It would indicate that the simple group was very popular, possibly because it was associated with the traditional 'Moon-viewing' Festival for the harvest moon. The plant cuttings used were kudsu vine, Chinese bell flower, thoroughwort, patrinia, pink, pampas grass (miscanthus) and bush clover. These plants are not available everywhere, but it is fun to search for substitutes in land, hedgerow or field, and to make a local 'seven autumnal plants' Ikebana.

The symbolism of materials

Most countries have a certain symbolism for their flowers. Denmark's national flower, the forget-me-not, is an instance, and we are familiar with the French symbolism of *pensées* — pansies for thoughts. Rather more symbolism is observed in Japan and great attention is given to colour significance also. Pink flowers suggest feminine gentleness and virtue and hence a happy choice for Mothering Sunday would be pink and white carnations. Mothers' Day is now celebrated in Japan.

For the New Year festivities the trio of pine, prunus and bamboo are traditional. The evergreen pine symbolises strength and long life. The prunus suggests the purity of women, stressing the virtues of fidelity and veracity because it survives the harsh winter tenaciously and blossom bursts forth even before winter has passed. Bamboo is noted for its resilience. Bending under the stresses of life's storms it never breaks, returning to its upright position when the wind has passed.

Peach blossom symbolises happiness in marriage. The delicate pink buds are associated with feminine beauty and virtue. It is invariably

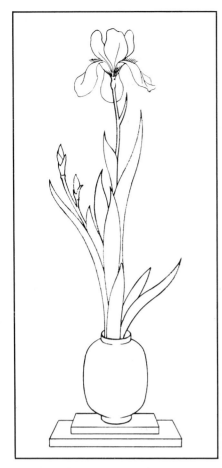

112 Classical *seika* of iris tectorum.

used in arrangements for the dolls' display on Girls' Day in March.

Cherry blossom symbolises perfection, and is the most popular of all flowers in Japan. Cherry blossom time is the Spring — a happy time and to be celebrated. Innumerable *haikus* have been written round the breath-taking beauty of the trees in blossom since the earliest times. It is rarely used for Ikebana on happy occasions, however, since the blossoms quickly fall signifying to the superstitious mind sudden death.

The peony originated in China and it symbolises prosperity and success. Throughout the ages its beauty has inspired Chinese and Japanese to paint it on screens and scrolls.

The iris symbolises upstanding manhood with all the virtues of valour and purity. The flat pointed leaves remind one of the warrior's sword. These leaves have a curved and a straight side and there is an etiquette in the manner of placing them, as is described later. Iris are very popular in all schools and there are many traditional ways of arranging them, each school having its individual technique.

Morning glory is not difficult to arrange. A long hanging stem looks best in a hanging arrangement with a short piece of medium length and then a flower and a bud for *hikae*. Sometimes the longest stem is wound round a short sprig of bamboo to lift it well off the edge of the container when a hanging arrangement is used. This use of morning glory is seldom seen outside Japan, possibly because the flower is so short-lived. A gourd is the favourite container for it, and because of the plant's prolific growth it has come to be known as 'the poor man's flower'.

Lotus, called in Japanese *hasu no hana*, symbolises a noble spirit and sincerity. These derive from Buddhism, hence the suggestion of purity rising above the mud of the pool where lie its roots. Usually it looks best in traditional arrangements, such as a cursive or *sô* style *seika* arrangement of the Ikenobo School. The lotus is used to illustrate the cosmic significance of time as applied to Ikebana. The seed pod represents the past, the opening flower is the present, and the bud with furled young leaves suggests the future. As these flowers usually open before dawn and close when the sun rises, one must get up early to see them in the natural state.

The 'seven autumnal plants', mentioned earlier, symbolise the coming of autumn when the harvest is in. The material is suitable for many styles of arrangement, classical or modern, and sometimes not all seven materials are used. In that case those of contrasting characteristics are chosen — for instance, cascading vine as a complement to upright grasses. This material is usually arranged in a basket container.

Immortality is symbolised by the chrysanthemum. From the twelfth century, the Imperial Court has used the emblem because it also represents peace and nobility of heart. It is thought to have been introduced from China in the eighth century. Today there are thousands of varieties, and cultivation is so profuse that robes and kimonos are made up entirely of flowers and put on life-size dolls of wicker and straw. The dolls are called *kikuningyo* and they are on exhibit during chrysanthemum time. The art of making these flower-robes is little more than a century old but is threatened with extinction because the apprentices are attracted to better-paid work in industry. It is said that an average of ten thousand blooms are necessary for one kimono for use in a *kabuki* play.

Maple symbolises the declining year. It is at its best with brilliant autumnal colours which are the perfect complement for tawny and golden-hued chrysanthemums.

113 Cherry blossom and white iris in
a pear-shaped stoneware *suiban*. The style
is variation 2, *risshin kei*.

114 LEFT: A two-tier arrangement of iris and cherry blossom in a *niju kiri* container of the type used by the Ikenobo School. Normally only one or two kinds of material are used for this type of arrangement. Here, pink double tulips have been added for colour as *nejime* in the upper level. Iris are often used in both upper and lower levels.

115 RIGHT: A small Chinese carved brown soapstone, vase, with three scarlet ranunculae on a matching lacquered base, is used for a right-hand *keishin kei* variation 2 arrangement.

The camellia closes the floral calendar for the year as it appears in December, like the last flicker of a flame, before dark skies and snow come. It has such striking beauty that it must be arranged with care and skill to show blooms and buds to best advantage.

Festivals and flowers
With their deep consciousness of floral symbolism and love of festivals, as well as pilgrimages to renowned beauty spots, it would be odd if there were not some sort of Japanese festival for every month of the year. Many festivals are regional, but all are family affairs and are unfortunately dying out — with the exception of those major festivals which are celebrated nationally. The two which appear to be most important are the Festival of Boys and that of Girls.

Hinamatsuri is the Girls' Festival, when Ikebana of peach blossoms are made and the occasion is celebrated with a display of beautiful dolls. These are not the everyday playthings of children but ceremonial dolls, often cherished heirlooms. This beautiful custom has survived from the seventh century. At that time the dolls were made of paper and were sent floating down the river afterwards as votive prayers for an auspi-

cious year to come. The *hinamatsuri* is a cherished festival because it knits family bonds and expresses the love and devotion of parents for their daughters. It is celebrated on the third day of the third lunar month.

On the fifth day of the fifth month, *tango-no-sekku*, the Boys' Festival, is celebrated. Originally it may be that the occasion was fixed to coincide with the iris blooming in May and June, as the Ikebana for the Festival is always done with iris — generally a simple *seika* style or 'fish-path' *moribana*. It is severely simple. The sword-like leaves are placed in separate groups which have been rearranged differently from natural growth. There are many complicated rules governing the arrangement of iris in *seika* style, and these are not for the beginner.

It may be remarked that three varieties of iris are commonly used: the Japanese iris (iris laevigata), the iris ensenata and the iris tectorum. When using the tectorum the blades should always be turned inward so that the hooked tip turns towards the main and tallest stem. The annual observance of Boys' Day promotes a consciousness of coming manhood with its obligations.

Between these two important festivals there is the Cherry Blossom Festival in April. Japan owes its epithet 'cherry blossom land' to its na-

116 OPPOSITE: This simple arrangement of
a gracefully curved grevillea stem with
bunched white chrysanthemums at the
centre represents the 'full moon'.

tional flower, which has been featured for centuries by poet and painter alike. Although so ephemeral, the blossom is esteemed as the symbol of the national spirit, typifying the patriotism of the ancient *samurai* (knights), who were often killed in battle. The introduction of the Festival is attributed to the Emperor Sago, who is reputed to have held the first cherry blossom viewing party in the year 812 AD.

There are some three hundred varieties of cherry, from the first-blooming small blossom, *higan zakura* to *yae zakura*, the last-blooming double variety. The Japanese poet Issa has immortalised cherry blossom in his well-known *haiku*:

> *Under the blossom*
> *Utter strangers*
> *Simply don't exist*

When Ellen Gordon Allen founded the world-wide association, Ikebana International, she had very clear vision. She wisely understood the blessings the this gentle art of Ikebana would bring to a world shattered by international strife, and possible threat of atomic extinction. She had in mind, I suspect, Issa's poem — the association's emblem is a spray of cherry blossom — and the idea that true friendship would be promoted and fostered by all peoples of the world through the practice of the art.

Another important festival is *Tanabata*, the Star Festival, which is also the festival of lovers and falls on the seventh day of the seventh month. We are all interested in the customs and culture of other nations, and the story of the legendary lovers Princess Shokuge and the handsome shepherd Kengyn is as lovely as, and resembles, that of Hero and Leander.

The daughter of the King of Heaven was a weaver, Princess Star (Vega), and she wove day after day intricate and beautiful robes befitting the illustrious king, until one day the handsome Kengyn (Aquila) passed by. Thereafter her attention to her work was neglected more and more. Their love grew and they plighted their troth, but the king, despairing for his supply of robes, angrily withheld his consent to their marriage and banished them eternally to opposite sides of the River of Heaven, *Amanagwa*, which we recognise as the Milky Way.

The tears of the Princess, however, melted her father's heart and, relenting, he permitted the lovers to meet once a year — on the seventh day of the seventh moon. Alas, when the time came for their meeting they found the river was too wide to cross. The bitter grief of the Princess won the sympathy of a magpie who marshalled a whole flock of magpies to build a bridge for the lovers to cross and be reunited.

The Festival was introduced from China during the Nara period (710-714). On the day of the Festival it was the custom to invoke the star Vega with votive offerings of flowers that girls might become skilful in weaving, sewing and the gentler arts. Nine centuries later, records show that the Festival was still celebrated, it being under Imperial patronage in 1629 when the Emperor Go-Mizu-no-o summoned Senko, the thirty-second Master of the Ikenobo School, to the palace to arrange an exhibition of *rikka* arrangements, the Emperor himself participating. Until 1905 the *Tanabata* Festivals were private, for lords, nobles and artists. They are now exhibitions open to the public. Today the annual displays and street decorations are like carnivals and show great imagination. In Sendai the colourful sight attracts visitors from all parts of Japan.

November brings the Chrysanthemum Festival. This national flower and symbol of immortality appears in all art because of its decorative

as well as its symbolistic character. We find it on scrolls, kimonos, screens, enamels, porcelain and lacquer ware.

Everywhere that this lovely flower is grown in any quantity there is an annual chrysanthemum show. These are particularly popular in Europe and the United States in autumn. One such that I found quite unforgettable was at Longwood Gardens, of the Dupont Foundation in Delaware. It must surely have no peer except in Japan.

In ancient times the Chrysanthemum Festival was also associated with the Moon-viewing Celebration. A picture scroll dated 1551 by Sen-ami, an Ikenobo master, shows early *rikka* style arrangements for the five annual festivals, the fifth being chrysanthemums for Moon-viewing.

4 How long does it take?

Fundamental structures for simple arrangements

There is no such thing as 'instant Ikebana', but contrary to general belief there are several arrangements the pattern of which, once learned, can be done in a very few minutes. Of these, the seventh variation of the Sogetsu School offers a trio of simple arrangements.

Morimono

This is an arrangement of fruit, or fruit and vegetables, with possibly a selected flower and some leaves or grasses. Either a basket, a polished board, a tray or a large leaf serves for a base in the design. The arranger should exercise restraint, as it is not a piled-up mass of material but rather a still-life picture suggesting the season. Close attention should be paid to harmony of colours and textures. It is one of the best exercises I know for developing one's taste and artistic ability. Choose colourful fruit in perfect condition. Apples should be polished, whether golden, rosy or green. Place two pieces of fruit off centre on the base, arranged so that if one is on its side the other is upright. The texture of apples looks well on a polished lacquer tray as the shine on the skin is in textural harmony. Apples suggest autumn, when nuts are also in season, and a nice contrast would be chestnut burrs — especially if they were about to burst, giving a glimpse of the mahogany sheen of the nut inside the burr. Walnuts could also be used, or purple plums, grapes, aubergines, or shiny green and red pimentoes. Even tomatoes give a good colour and texture note. The flower, if one is used, should be of the season also and not too conspicuous. Bronze-hued small chrysanthemums are very suitable, but the addition of a flower or two introduces a problem. What about water? If the *morimono* is for display during a few hours only, it does not matter. On the other hand, if one is concerned that the bloom will wilt, it should be impaled on a small *kenzan* in a low pot of water or preferably a '*well-kenzan*' — which is a combined holder and pot. Whatever is used should be hidden by leaves or berries in a cluster. The choice of flower is thus governed by the necessity for a bloom to retain a fresh look for at least a few hours. An hydrangea stands up well without water for a short while and is available in a choice of beautifully soft colours ranging from blue to purple and rose. It takes on pastel shades of green as it dries out, and is most attractive.

Ukibana

The second of the trio of the seventh variation has the delightful Japanese name *ukibana*, meaning floating flowers. These, being cut very short and close to the head, need less depth of container, and a large tray or plate will often serve. Again, a lacquer tray is most suitable,

117 ABOVE: Very popular for people who lead busy lives are 'moon arrangements'. This shows an opening lily in a moon-shaped container which can be hung or stood. The symbolism is the 'waxing moon'. See also *plates 116, 119* and *132*.

118 BELOW: *Ukibana* with two deep red gladioli blooms and a few stems of teased leaves cut short. The container is a Chinese dish resembling a fluted leaf on a stem. The characteristic design on the porcelain has prunus blossom and a butterfly, the omen of happiness. To anchor this floating group the smallest possible *kenzan* is used.

being plain and in one colour. Black is much favoured, as is gold, but coloured trays are perfectly suitable — although they impose the need to choose flower colours carefully. Do not overlook the additional possibility of using a silver bowl or crystal dish if the *ukibana* is for a formal dinner table.

If one is ambitious, and requires something large for display on a side table or a table in the centre of a large room, two lacquer trays or low bowls can be used. Contrast of colour makes a most interesting arrangement as, for instance, a black tray used with an olive-green one. One tray would contain two flowers and the other a single bloom. Full-grown roses, medium chrysanthemums or dahlias are effective. Another possibility is three flowers from a stem of gladioli joined like a trefoil. When using a pair of bowls or trays, they should be semi-united with trails of fern or creeper; and, if it is autumn, vines with berries can be used.

The whole purpose of *ukibana* is to convey a feeling of refreshment, and this is done by leaving a good deal of the water visible. If one is fortunate enough to have a lily pond in the garden there is clearly no better choice of flowers for *ukibana*, but they require a large bowl to preserve scale. The Japanese would choose a plain lacquer bowl about fifteen inches in diameter and coloured black or midnight blue. The dark colours intensify the reflections in the water and so suggest tranquility. My favourite *ukibana* bowl, used only when I can obtain pink peach-blossom, is a precious Chinese-style ceramic made by a gifted modern potter. The pale turquoise glaze is an inspiration and, the inverted cone being too small for lilies or even camellias, it is perfect for the tiny buds on a short spray intended to suggest the tip of a sapling seen against the evening sky.

For those who rarely see peach-blossom there are 'wind flowers' — which the ancient Greeks so loved and immortalised with the beautiful name meaning 'alone in the wind' — anemones. These are ideal for *ukibana*. The pascal hellibore flowers, which with all the coaxing imaginable (even a drink of alcohol!) hang their heads so drowsily, are best arranged in *ukibana* style. If one wishes to simulate the water-lily leaf, the smaller megasea leaves are excellent and they combine with hellibore very well. And, of course, one should always remember the camellias when they are in season.

Shikibana

No container or base is required for *Shikibana*, meaning 'spread flowers'. It is designed for short periods of display as might be required to honour a visitor or decorate a dinner table. It has been a popular table decoration in India and Pakistan, as well as the Far East, for a long time and possibly originated in India. I have even seen *shikibana* in a Dubrovnik hotel, where a head waiter with imagination decorated a banquet table with sprigs of myrtle and short-stemmed flowers. Carnations and zinnias are very suitable for this type of arrangement. I have also seen most attractive *shikibana* in a West Country fair, where clematis was used effectively to meet the schedule for a 'tea table decoration' centrepiece. It is thus quite a universal style.

The Japanese *shikibana* conforms to the rules for basic arrangements of three main stems — *shin*, *soe* and *hikae*. Instead of being upstanding branches and flowers, the material rests on the table and points in three directions so that it may be viewed from all sides. The three main stems divide the space fairly equally so that there is an angle of 120 degrees

between each stem. As in basic arrangements, the second and third
stems are related in proportion to the longest stem. The overall size of
the arrangement would be decided by the size of the table width. Sprays
of asparagus fern, or smilax, are pretty, and flowering quince can also
be used in this way. Most of us can get tree ivy easily, and it is particularly suited for *shikibana*, especially with the bunches of berries, but it
should be remembered that all the material must be kept fairly low.

One of the most effctive *shikibana* I have ever seen was done by my
wife for supper tables when we lived in South America and had many
sub-tropical plants in our garden. Buds of scarlet hibiscus were gathered
the evening before they were required and placed in a polythene bag, in
the refrigerator, for twenty-four hours. Fifteen minutes before sitting
down to supper the buds were laid decoratively on the table amid sprays
of suitable leaves which had been prepared for them. The guests, as
they came to table and noticed the buds, invariably remarked, 'What

120 LEFT: A large blue-black Japanese lacquer *suiban* is used for this Ichiyo School arrangement of pine and old-gold chrysanthemums. A large expanse of water reflects the pine admirably.

121 RIGHT: This is a free style design based on variation 4. The single pink rose, low down in a grey ceramic bowl is *hikae*, and a plume of bleached broom tinted the same colour is *shin*.

a pity hibiscus closes at night'. However, they were utterly amazed within a few minutes as the flowers would start unfolding, and soon they would be full-blown in their delayed dawn loveliness. This is the practice in Hawaii where my wife had learnt the secret.

In the West the tempo of our lives in recent years has so speeded up that few people feel they have time to arrange the flowers carefully and they just put them in fresh water in an attractive vase. Even that takes ten minutes. Well, Ikebana can be done just as quickly! Tokyo has out-placed us in the pursuit of speed. Flower Master Meikof Kasuya, Head-master of the Ichiyo School, has specialised in the simplification of train-ing and he has devised, for busy housewives, some quick Ikebana designs which are charming in their simplicity.

The Ichiyo School has six fundamental styles, the third of which is known as the 'short stem' style. It is described here, as it seems ideal for anyone who has never before attempted to 'do the flowers'.

(The six fundamental styles of the Ichiyo School are: upright, slanting, flat or short stem style, four-view or table centre style, *nageire* slanting style and *nageire* hanging or cascade style).

Short stem arrangement

This Ichiyo design, *moribana* style, was shown by Mr. Kasuya when he visited London during his world tour in 1966. It can be completed in a few minutes and has the advantage that it can be displayed on a side table or used as a table centre.

It is a very flat arrangement, the low bowl being of any size and shape, round, oval or rectangular, but the oval shape seems best suited as it shows more water. It is only necessary to remember to keep the arrangement in scale. Unless the bowl is twelve inches or more wide, small flowers must be used, such as sprays of 'pom-pom' chrysanthemums. Two *kenzans* are required, and the 'sun and moon' couple are best. One part — the 'moon' — is placed to the rear and well to one side, either left or right, while the 'sun' component is placed to the front toward the opposite side of the bowl, but nearer the centre-line. The material is arranged asymmetrically in the two *kenzans*, roughly in the proportions of two-thirds for 'sun' and one-third for 'moon'. The flowers should always be shorter than the branch material, the tallest piece being less than half the diameter of the bowl. Three pieces of foliage and three blooms (or bunches of small flowers) are usually sufficient, but supporting pieces of foliage will often improve the design. A plain bowl looks

122 *Heishin kei*. For a chalice-type vase horizontal arrangements are best. *Hikae* is a flower supported by two others, and as is usual when using pussy-willow, supporting stems are necessary for *shin* and *soe*.

best and does not detract from the beauty of the flowers. Materials suggested are pine with roses, dahlias, carnations or chrysanthemums. Some small varieties added to medium-sized blooms add to the beauty of the arrangement. Bushy sprigs of heather also look pretty whether or not they are in bloom. Because pine has natural curves, it can be placed with the bowed lines curving inward, instead of drooping and giving a depressing mood. A piece of driftwood may be used to partially bridge the gap between the two *kenzans*, but the gap should never be quite closed. To create a tranquil feeling, at least one third of the water surface should be visible. It is also well to remember the classic tradition that in summer the water level is high, whereas in winter it is low.

Ikebana reflects the busy world in which we live today, and it is quite in order to have very simple and quickly-made arrangements. One of

123 A free style arrangement, based on variation 2, in a dull black chalice-type vase, using sprays of white blossom and purple buddleia. The long *shin* line is on the right, *soe* almost upright and *hikae* suggests a spray growing over a wall.

124 LEFT: A left-hand *nageire* arrangement, *keishin kei* variation 3, showing how spatial balance is attained despite the assymetrical placement of material. The three main stems are branches of medlar and the *jushis* are massed white roses.

126 RIGHT: This *nageire* arrangement of autumn tinted hawthorn branches and small yellow chrysanthemums is based on *keishin kei* variation 1. the three main stems being of branches and part of *hikae* filling the space between itself and *soe*. The tall container is a celadon glazed 'two-piece' vase designed by the author and thrown by Kay Pritchett.

125 LEFT: Another *heishin kei* in a chalice-type tall vase using wistaria vines for *shin* and its supporters, the third supporter coming forward to give depth. Two leaves of bocconia cordata are used for *soe* and, for balance, two heads of light and dark blue hydrangea break the line of the cup rim. The *tomi* of purple berberis berries, with their bloom still on them, makes an attractive colour composition in the dull grey container.

92

the charms of Ikebana is its simplicity and 'uncontrived' look. Led by the principal Flower Masters of the great Tokyo schools, one follows their interpretations of exciting forms and designs. This is not copying because one can never have exactly the same material or container. Often a master will tell his pupil the source of an inspiration. Mr. Kasuya is fond of citing the visit to Tokyo, many years ago, of the great ballerina Anna Pavlova and his first impressions of ballet from the West, which led him to develop space-enclosing lines in his designs. One is reminded of the linear composition not only of 'Les Sylphides' but also of the paintings of Degas. He interprets the beauty of movement with what he calls 'dancing lines'. The Flower Masters of Tokyo are great artists with a life-time of dedication behind them, so that their teachers follow the patterns or styles which they produce. So too should the pupil, who should also keep a book of drawings with details of all arrangements made. In this way time-consuming trial and error is avoided because one goes straight ahead, knowing exactly what one is going to do, and — what is more important — knowing that the result will look right.

Perhaps working from a pattern of form may take a little longer on the first attempt, but thereafter the design can be repeated, using different flowers and foliage, in very little time. Having learned the first 'quick arrangement', the beginner proceeds to the next and soon builds up a repertoire.

It is wise to acquire the two essential types of container for *moribana* and *nageire* arrangements as soon as possible. I suggest having matching or definite contrast — such as black and white — as in either case they can be used together for the series of combination arrangements described in the Sogetsu eighth variation.

Modern potters, well aware of flower arrangers' needs today, are producing more pots suitable for Ikebana. At all big flower exhibitions there are sales tables with the right types of container for Ikebana both as regards shape and also types of glaze. The china and glass departments of big stores, and also some agents for our better-known china and glass ware manufacturers, have a wide selection. Many enthusiasts decide to take advantage of the splendid facilities created by local authorities to teach pottery making. Such facilities are to be found in most cities where evening classes are held in arts and various handicrafts. One then has the additional enjoyment of a second creative outlet under the skilled guidance of a tutor. It takes time to learn to throw a pot, but coiled and moulded pots are less demanding in skill and time.

It has been found that there is a short cut for the *nageire* type of tall vase arrangements avoiding the technique of fixing (which may bother students at first). It is the use of a chalice-shaped vase on a tall stem or column; the cup will hold a *kenzan* which is so much easier for fixing branches and flowers. The shape is graceful too, reminding one of ancient Chinese stem-cups, and they can be used for pedestal-like arrangements as well as Ikebana. Such arrangements are suited to our western interiors, whether they be Regency or contemporary in style.

In all schools *nageire* style arrangements are almost invariably asymmetrical and they will be successful as long as one bears in mind the principle of 'balance', by which is meant not only mechanical balance but also spatial balance — that is, having a large mass to balance a long out-reaching main stem. The mass part need not necessarily be a large leaf or group but one can suggest shape by using a vine and so enclosing a void. The outline of mass is one of illusory mass and weightlessness.

127 An arrangement suggesting a lakeside view. Pine and orange coloured tulips combine well in an upright arrangement, using a modern black and pale green ceramic by George Wilson.

94

5 What does it cost?

Economy, transience and representation

There are three reasons why Ikebana is rapidly gaining universal popularity. It is economical, ephemeral and nonrepresentational. Few flowers are used so that a big expenditure is not necessary to achieve a work of floral art. The material fades and within a week one is creating new beauty. The banality of living indefinitely with an arrangement is avoided. A talented painter or sculptor might create a great work of art at the cost of exhausting effort and some expense. But, whatever its merit, one might tire of living with it. There is an antipathy to physical permanence in art except when there is a monetary basis. This goes hand in hand with a praiseworthy revulsion from representational art. One just leaves that to the camera — and there is a tendency to regard photography as merely a means of communication; but it is also geneally recognised that in the hands of a competent person there is an art in photography too.

Our restless spirits crave change, and Ikebana affords just that. Ikebana can, of course, be interpretive in a widely evocative way. The insistence of water being visible in some arrangements is intended to induce a feeling of coolness and refreshment, especially in the hot summers of Japan.

The underlying concept of heaven, man and earth, deriving from the impulse to suggest a landscape, or even the universe in traditional *rikka* arrangements, is present in all schools. It is achieved, however, by an economy of means which is astonishing. A small bough, a stone or some pebbles and a few simple wild flowers in a bowl of water can bring into the smallest of homes a lakeside view. This training of the imaginative faculty is only one of the benefits which may be derived from continued practice of Ikebana.

Urban overcrowding, in Tokyo particularly, does not generally permit the enjoyment of even the small garden which we often take for granted in our cities and suburbs. The carefully devised substitute of the Japanese home is the miniature landscape or garden which is either provided by an Ikebana arrangement, *bonzai* (dwarf trees), or *bonseki* (tray landscapes).

The Japanese are a naturally thrifty race because of their established economy and the fact that in their country the rewards of labour are not, by our standards, very high. One can only give credit to, and have admiration for, the clever solution to their problem of lack of space and their instinctive insistence of beauty both in their homes and in their lives.

It follows quite naturally that in Japan florists are legion and they sell everything from flowers to foliage and grasses for Ikebana — not

128 A slanting *nageire*
arrangement of peony buds,
a medlar branch having a
strong upward sweep,
and three bocconia cordata
leaves for *hikae* are arranged
in a tall stoneware vase.
The mass of the bocconia
leaves is a good balance
for the long *shin* line.

129 Using an Ichiyo School
mottled blue glazed
'U-shaped' container
designed by Meikof Kasuya
the Headmaster, cherry
blossom and a camellia
bud appear to be bending
gently in a Spring breeze.

in bunches of half-dozens or dozens but by the piece. Happily, the 'dozen to a bunch' practice is — thanks to the demands of flower arrangers everywhere — being changed, although somewhat reluctantly, by florists.

The importance of containers

Ikebana only becomes expensive when one is confronted with the temptation to acquire some rare and beautiful container. It is not necessary to rush out to sale rooms for Chinese and Japanese ceramics, nor to haunt antique dealers, coveting a celadon vase. The cost of such items would, in any case, make them far too precious for regular use owing to risk of breakage. If feeling extravagant, by all means indulge in the purchase of a bronze container that cannot break. (I always enjoy the glow of satisfaction when recalling that I found my nineteenth century *usubata* in the 'flea market' of Nice many years ago and bought it for the proverbial 'song'. At the same time I regret bitterly that I did not buy other pieces then offered but now unobtainable, except at greatly inflated cost.)

One must be prepared to spend a reasonable sum of money on containers, but as Sofu Teshigahara says, 'the good arranger will always find something interesting among daily table-ware'. Summer arrangements require baskets, and any simple bread-basket will serve with a *well-kenzan*.

As one progresses, and the scope of design which can be attempted is extended, it might be wise to consider the advantages of lacquer ware, especially from the breakage angle. Lacquer bowls are now freely imported from Japan and are available in a London Ikebana shop, as well as the United States, where Ikebana is rather more universal. Some Japanese Flower Masters design their own lacquer vases and bowls. The colours cover a wide range and such containers are very pleasing because of their lustre, lending themselves admirably to *moribana* arrangements. Should the polished surface become dulled with use, due to scratches, restoration can often be effected by rubbing with common brass polish. It must be applied with discretion and only after a trial rub on the underside of the bowl as such polish is mildly abrasive. Suitable lacquer containers are available at slightly less cost than ceramics imported from Japan, but like them, since they are also imported, the price is affected by customs duty.

One can devise 'do-it-yourself' containers for very much less cost and this type is discussed in detail later.

Collecting containers

Containers are, therefore, of first importance. Often a vase will inspire the arranger, although I usually find that it is the flowers which suggest the use of a particular container. We are all aware that roses call for silver and crystal, and it is interesting to observe that, obsessed with an admiration for our lovely Western flowers, the Japanese are now, with characteristic artistry, manufacturing glassware for the Ikebana market. We must not be inhibited about the type of container for Ikebana, especially with roses. These can be arranged in any of the basic styles and their variations in Venetian, Scandinavian or Italian glass as well as classic crystal. (It is as well to remember that if a *kenzan* is used it may be seen through the glass. A useful substitute holder in such a container is glass marbles, or alternatively, one can wrap the kenzan carefully in foil or white tissue paper.)

132 LEFT: This classical full-moon arrangement illustrates the charm of combining roses and pine in the burnished copper 'moon-container' which can either be hung or placed on a plinth.

A greater fluency of expression in floral art is possible when there is a battery of containers to choose from. Each container should have an adhesive label on the bottom with its number, and records should be kept in a booklet. Over a period of many years I have acquired something approaching one hundred containers. There the number is likely to stop, for I discard containers frequently and there are occasional breakages, as well as sales, to afford me the opportunity to acquire new items. This statement might perhaps alarm the beginner, so here I should emphasise that one shallow dish and one tall vase will enable anyone to go quite a long way.

Many of my containers are my own over-ambitious ceramic experiments (which have failed because I am but the veriest amateur potter). I do it simply to acquaint myself with the technical possibilities so that I may design for more skilful potters to make what I require. My collection includes a rare family piece, which has come down to me through several generations. It is a Bavarian glass goblet delicately etched and tinted and is only used on special occasions at home. The goblet calls for special flowers, such as miniature roses, carnations or smaller flowers of fairy-like beauty such as lily of the valley. There is also a crackle-ware Japanese *suiban* dish of the nineteenth century. Possibly it once held a *bonzai* tree growing on a mossy rock, but I found it some years ago in the potting shed of a Japanese florist in Lima, Peru. It was being used as a drip tray for pots of seedlings and I suspect the owner did not know what it was because he practically gave it to me with a bouquet of flowers which I bought.

In Ikebana, harmony can only be achieved by full compatibility between container and the line and length of material used. The position of the flowers and the colour scheme may be changed to suit the surroundings. A wide-mouthed container should not be rejected because it presents difficulties of fitting a cross-bar support. It is quite in order to use bushy material placed in a low position as support for branches and flowers. Care must be taken, however, to avoid completely covering the mouth of the vase, so that 'the flowers may breathe', as a Japanese Flower Master would say.

Although dimensional and proportional characteristics have been stressed for basic arrangements and the eight variations described earlier, it is an accepted practice in 'free-style' to make small, but not miniature, arrangements in which the volume of floral material is not more than one half of the volume of the vase. However this does not always appeal to Western taste but such an arrangement can be both arresting and very beautiful if expertly done.

Boxes and covered bowls with lids removed and resting against the side are used in the Sogetsu School for free-style arrangements and they are particularly suited to the fourth variation — the style of omission — where the single flower is placed low as *hikae* and the lid serves to conceal the *kenzan*.

Never be afraid of very large containers because of the technical problem of fixture which might be involved. Large branches should be nailed together to meet this difficulty, making certain that the nails do not show. This makes a foundation of branches which facilitates the arranging of flowers without fixture aids.

Similarly one should not discard a small but impressive container. Often it is a perfect complement for a sweeping but light design arranged in an airy fashion.

It is a part of the Sogetsu School training to make objects of iron, stone (such as pumice and soft limestone), as well as wood, for use as stands or containers. Calligraphy is not overlooked and all of this contributes to the making of the artist. One such object consisted of chopsticks lacquered black and loosely bunched so that the ends fanned outwards. Such sheaves could be done with split bamboo, reeds or aluminium rods welded together. With this strange form, globes of massed flowers, fresh or dried, seed pods or even coloured plastic scouring pads could be used. This is, of course, the threshold of sculpture.

Making your own containers
Everyone who has discovered the joys of Ikebana should, sooner or later, exercise the imagination by devising a do-it-yourself container. Much profit will stem from the various discoveries made and a few suggestions which follow will serve as signposts and basic ideas to work on independently. As mentioned earlier, a milk bottle, concealed by a reed mat, is within the scope of every student. Bear in mind that simplicity of form and texture are essential in successful experiments. Some people are more imaginative, or technically skilful, than others, so that it is sometimes best to work as a pair or small team. Family and friends could be asked for ideas and enjoy the fun of putting them into effect. The necessary tools are quite minimal, and are usually found in the odd-job box of tools of most homes.

If obtainable, sheet lead can be hammered into attractive bowls or shallow box-like containers — using either a cigar box or block of wood as a former. For rounder shapes, an upturned wooden salad bowl can be tried. The mallet technique is soon acquired by trial and error, but if a hammer is used a ball-pane or rounded end is advisable. The small pits of metal hammer-marks are decorative texture and common in most hand-wrought metal work.

The weight and cost of lead restrict this method to rather small containers, but the work is well justified for the lovely pewter effect obtained. An anvil and some skill are, however, necessary to work sheet copper and only those who have had a little training should attempt such work.

What may appear to be a hideous ceramic vase or bowl, because of its poor taste in decoration, can be transformed into a very useful vessel at the smallest expense. Silver paint to which some black matt (blackboard paint) has been added will transform even a glass instant coffee jar into what looks like dull pewter. I have seen a soup plate so transformed and used with begonias in flame colours most effectively. It should, however, be pointed out that once so treated or sprayed any reversion to the original state would be difficult. So look for suitability first. Is the dish or bowl deep enough to use a *kenzan*? Then study the form. Is there the necessary simplicity of shape and line? Finally, examine the surface. Any raised decoration will generally disqualify a container unless it is of a geometrical character.

An easy conversion is to take a tall biscuit tin of cylindrical shape with rounded corners and to apply lengths of split bamboo, sticks or reeds to the surface (excellent cellulose adhesive agents are marketed complete with instructions). The sticks (or whatever is used) should be cut to size before making the bond, and the interior of the tin sprayed or painted as an anti-corrosive measure. An alternative cover is horizontal strips of plastic (see *plates 143-4*).

134 LEFT: The vase shown is very suitable for a *seika* style arrangement of two dark green aspidistra leaves, the foremost of which shows the underside of the leaf, and two pink tulips having gracefully curved lines of leaves.

135 RIGHT: This yellow Chinese pot with raised decoration in colour, showing lotus and a crane, is very suited for a right-hand basic *risshin kei* arrangement of forsythia as it repeats the exact colour of the rather ornate jar. The symbolism of the aquatic plants on the jar, since they would yield to the movement of water, suggests that we should adapt ourselves to changing times. The crane symbolises freedom – especially when shown in flight.

136 LEFT: Japanese crackle-ware *suiban* used for a 'fish-path' double arrangement. *Hikae* is a stone of interesting form.

137 RIGHT: Massed daffodils and grape hyacinth give the required brilliant colour contrast for this Spring arrangement in which salix tortuosa is used for the *shin* line, *soe* being a part of the same branch.

138 This old Japanese *suiban* in ivory
crackle-ware is most suitable for a slanting
Spring arrangement using pink hyacinth
and a branch of flowering currant.

The most satisfactory do-it-yourself containers are, of course, ceramics
and often the most simple forms are very charming indeed. The Japanese *raku* pots for drinking tea are fascinating to make and easily wrought.
A small ball of clay is held in the left hand and then gradually shaped
by using the right thumb and turning the clay continuously until the
gently curved cup-shape is obtained.

I strongly recommend any flower arranger to take a course of pottery
at one of the nearby day or evening classes arranged by the local education authority. The tactful guidance of the tutor steers one clear of
the commonest pitfalls of wrong technique in shaping, texturing and

139 RIGHT: This shows the upper section of the two-piece container, shaped like a 'compote', for a tall upright arrangement.

140 A two-piece celadon glazed container designed to take a *kenzan* in the upper section, for stable placement of branches and flowers. In this upright arrangement the *hikae* is a spray of deep pink chrysanthemums with bunched white ones supporting it behind and adding depth.

142 RIGHT: In this basic *risshin kei*, *hikae* is a rose with supporters while *shin* and *soe* are branches of blossom. The container is black and green celadon glazed, the outer surface being textured by a piece of date palm fibre. Designed and made by the author.
141 Free style of bamboo stems and tawny chrysanthemums based on *risshin kei* variation 2. The bowl is a Peruvian decorated gourd of which the keyed lid forms *tomi*.

143 and 144 Any tin that does not have sharp corners may be converted to make a container. Plate 144 shows how this has been done using semi-circular plastic strip table edging as used with formica-topped tables.

glazing, as well as helping to form one's taste.

It is in texturing that one encounters the greatest thrills of discovery. A length of twisted wire patted against the clay while it is still soft can suggest rain. Combing the surface with the teeth of a broken hacksaw blade produces, after suitable glazing, a sheen like watered silk. Stippling with a wire brush which is used for cleaning suede will give the effect of rough leather and needs no glaze. Patting a piece of open-weave dish-cloth against the clay with the back of a wooden spoon will result in a bark effect. These, and a thousand other pieces of 'bric-à-brac' to be found around every home, will produce exciting results in the hands of an imaginative student.

Incised design is generally for the expert who has become enamoured of Chinese celadon-ware and perfected his pottery technique to attempt copies. One can try, however, tracing a simple design and fastening it to the surface of a pot. Using a ball point pen sufficient impression can be made for subsequent guidance with a sharp tool used to incise the pattern. The clay should be in a 'leather-hard' condition so that it will not crumble under the pressure of incising.

There is no limit to inventiveness. Using clay rolled out like pastry one

145 LEFT: An abstract arrangement using pampas grass and plumes, contorted dried palm leaf and chrysanthemums. The material might suggest clouds and thundery showers. A carved wooden base is used to balance the teased grasses.

146 RIGHT: An abstract ceramic pot, modelled by the author and textured by stippling with a wire brush to suggest the surface of rough leather, is used for another version of variation 4.

can make all sorts of simple shapes. The beginner will be delighted with his results. The study of pottery will undoubtedly lead to greater interest in centuries-old pottery techniques, from the time when Neolithic man first made his eating, drinking and cooking pots about the third millenium BC, to the exquisite porcelains which were fashioned by Chinese, Korean and Japanese potters.

Inspiration can then be derived from well-illustrated books on the subject and visits to the magnificent national collections in museums. One

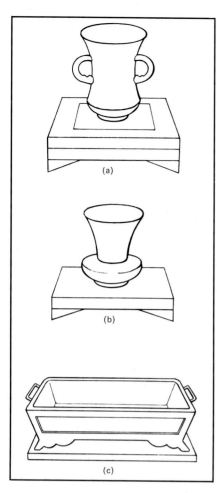

147 (a) 'Formal' *rikka* vase. (b) 'Semi-formal' *rikka* vase called *rikka hei*. (c) 'Informal' *rikka* vase or *sunabachi*.

soon learns that simplest shapes are loveliest and most are fashioned from commonplace objects (such as gourds), which are found in nature. The Chinese wine-cup is the prototype of what today is called in flower-arrangement jargon 'a compote' — meaning a bowl on some sort of base or stem. The lifting of a bowl or dish from the supporting surface seems to add grace and lightness to an arrangement, hence the popularity of 'pedestal' arrangements in Western floral art.

Classical, bronze and bamboo containers

In classical Ikebana, by which I refer to the last three centuries, the receptacles were never ornate nor extravagant in style. Whether of bronze or bamboo, the containers were always of simple form, and porcelains were sparsely decorated. The mouths of all receptacles were wide to allow a large surface of water to be exposed to oxygen in the air, thus keeping the water fresh.

Such a container is the *usubata* — with an upper part in the form of a tray and a central deep well which sits in the neck of the vase. The ends of stems are fixed in the well with a Y-shaped fork of twig and a brace cross-piece completing the *kubari*. When water is put in so that the tray is nearly full, there is a charming illusion of a tall arrangement rising from a lake.

The informal *rikka* arrangements were done in a rectangular low bowl usually made of bronze and having animalistic designs for legs. Frogs, birds in flight and dragons' claws were employed as motifs. Quite the loveliest arrangements for such precious containers would be those of the lotus. Land as well as water plants were used with moss-covered rock for these microcosmic arrangements. But for the informal *rikka* arrangement a board was rested on the lip of the bowl called *sunabachi*, meaning sand-bowl. This hid the water below it and carried sprinkled sand, giving the effect of the whole complicated arrangement rising from the earth. *Sunabachi* are rare pieces today but are sometimes simulated with cast-iron mouldings. These imitations should, however, be avoided because they will ultimately rust.

Concurrently with bronze pieces for the nobles came the simple bamboo containers evolved specifically for various styles by the great Flower Masters of the seventeenth century. Wood was also used frequently and these containers always had separate water-holders fitted, water being injurious to the bamboo and wood. Some of these formal vases were: *zundo*, or plain tubular type of bamboo; this was usually hung from the ceiling and used for simple cascade arrangements. The *tachi zuru* was a bamboo tall vase cut out in such a way that it resembled a 'standing crane'. Bamboo was also used for the classical boat arrangements called *tomari fune*, boat at anchor, and *tsuri fune*, or boat under way. This last had two meanings — homeward bound and outward bound. The symbolism was charming as the first was a welcome for the returning traveller and the second was to wish a departing guest 'fair winds' and a good journey. The 'boat' was fashioned quite simply by oblique cutting of the bamboo to suggest bow and prow of the vessel. These also were hanging arrangement containers whereas the 'boat at anchor' usually stood on a raft of bamboo. The symbolism here was, of course, a peaceful and quiet eventide in harbour after the day's labour.

Other bamboo vessels included the *niju kiri*, a graceful two-tiered container cut near the root of the tree so that the base was gnarled and showed the knots from which roots sprang. It was used for informal *seika*

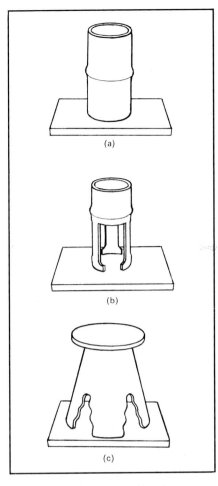

148 (a) *Zundo* (tubular vase of bamboo).
(b) *Tachi zuru* ('standing crane' bamboo).
(c) *Ogencho* ('black boar', bronze).

149 RIGHT: This traditional type of bamboo
double container, used by the Ikenobo
School, is known as *niju kiri* and is here
shown with a two-level arrangement.
The lower one of clivia with curved leaves
having strong lines and the upper one of
bright blue grape hyacinths, bunched in
front of a branch of windswept willow.
Colour and lines might suggest
a breezy Spring day.

arrangements with great effect. Then there was the *shishi-guchi-gata* or lion's mouth shape as the cutting resembled an open mouth. The *ryo mado gata* had a 'window' cut out of back and front somewhat like the lower part of the *niju kiri*. The records of these vessels with drawings by the ancient Masters have fortunately been preserved for centuries. They emphasise the fact that elaborate containers are not essential. During the last century tall *nageire* pots have been carved from bamboo trunk. Some of them are both exquisitely carved and highly polished. They have the

150 (a) *Niju kiri* ('two tiered' bamboo).
(b) and (c) *Shishi gushi gata*
(lion's mouth shape, bamboo).

(a)　　　(b)　　　(c)

disadvantage that the bamboo inevitably splits with age, but if one is lucky enough to obtain such a vase it is, of course, an easy matter to have some sort of a water container made (or to find a convenient glass jar) to fit inside the bamboo sheath.

Basket containers
Japanese wood-block prints of great beauty have come down to us from the seventeenth century and show that baskets, either for hanging or standing, were popular in China and Japan. It would seem that the Chinese used elaborate porcelain delicately ornamented and shaped. These baskets of flowers inspired poets whose verses were printed in Chinese characters as an integral part of the wood-block print, so that they too have survived.

We may assume that basket arrangements were favoured for Summer and perhaps Autumn arrangements as they afforded a pleasing harmony when grasses were used in them. Examples are shown overleaf.

151 (a) *Eboshi gata* (cap-shaped hanging container, bamboo.) (b) *Shaku-hachi* (flute shaped hanging container, bamboo.)
(c) *Ryo mado gata*: bamboo. These are unusual but attractive, usually used for the tea ceremony. They have a 'window' at back and front.
The flute shaped (b) sometimes has a hole in the side for a spray of camellia or a single flower.

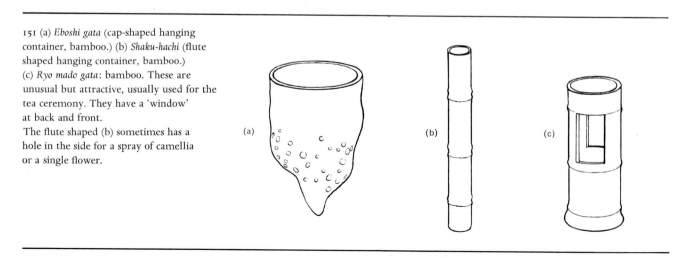

(a)　　　(b)　　　(c)

The skill of Japanese basket weavers is well known and their products are but one more testimony of the artistry that is innate in the whole race. The raw material has, of course, a most pleasing texture, the outer bark or skin being highly glossy and the fibres of the cane being exceedingly strong and easily bent.

I have used osier baskets which shepherds, on the slopes of the White Mountains in Crête, make to drain their cheeses. While these simple baskets do not have the fine finish of the oriental article, they look charming with mountain grasses and wild flowers.

The West has imported the baskets from many countries for practical holding purposes, especially for rolls and bread. These are perfectly suitable, as well as inexpensive, for *moribana* type arrangements.

The wicker used for weaving baskets can also be used for the looped whorls often added to modern arrangements and which seem to have come to stay, largely on account of their symbolism, because they imply 'happy return' in relation to seasons and persons. Prettier than wicker is the stripped weeping willow which, when fresh-cut, has a most attractive warm green hue.

Not to be despised is the common fish-trap found in some countries where one might spend a holiday. The lobster pots and crab pots with which we are familiar are rather heavy and huge, whereas the smaller wicker and reed traps are much more suitable because of lightness and unfamiliarity. The overall shape is that of a round bowl, and it is this mass which has to be considered when designing an arrangement. Reeds and grasses are again most suitable, and a delightful effect of 'being contained' is interpreted if a *well-kenzan* is used inside the trap with a single, but striking, bloom like a large rose, a brilliant camellia or a large flame coloured chrysanthemum.

Gourds should not be overlooked either. These are obtainable all through the Mediterranean and were used centuries ago by the Japanese who discovered the use of the 'sausage-shaped' gourd for *kakebana*, or wall arrangement. Ceramists have copied the shape of gourds, especially the waisted variety, from time immemorial. The vine producing the gourds is often used as an awning for shade in semi-tropical climates, and the gourds form convenient vessels for all kinds of liquid in primitive communities. Sometimes the gourds are decorated with a red-hot wire and these folk-craft boxes have perfectly fitting lids cut out and keyed so that they will fit only one way.

Bases

Most classical and traditional arrangements were set off with a suitable base, just as a picture is framed. One of the commonest and attractively simple stands was the *nakidai* with ends rolled under it.

Short-legged table type bases — in polished, often ornately-carved and sometimes red-lacquered, wood — were used with *rikka* and *seika* arrangements. This type of base is called *kwadai* as distinct from the boards, used in slats or large rectangles, in irregular shapes suggesting water pools, and also bamboo 'rafts' which were known as *shiki-ita*, or the generic term *dai*.

One classical bronze container — the *usubata* — has, as a rule, an integral three-legged base. It is used with a *kwadai*, however, as is another three-legged bronze vase known as *ogencho* or 'black boar'. One of the three legs is always placed toward the viewer and the other two legs at the back when setting up these containers with the *seika* arrangements

152 LEFT: Since the sixth century the Chinese have used baskets for flower arrangement, as shown on the end papers of this book. The Japanese used their incomparable artistry and skill to weave bamboo baskets. Here osier baskets are used because they harmonise well with the wild flowers and grasses found on the mountains of Crête, where this type of basket is used for draining the whey and making cheeses. A length of looped pine root is used to symbolise the return of Summer.

153 ABOVE LEFT: A fish-trap of wicker surrounds iris buds standing in a small bowl on a matching dark green lacquer base, to create an interesting free style arrangement.

154 ABOVE RIGHT: A bright coloured rose is contained in a fish trap while dried grasses soar upwards towards space. This is an abstract arrangement contrasting material and spiritual desires.

for which they were designed. This is an age-old etiquette still observed whenever such a container is used.

Wall tablets

The traditional *kakebana*, wall arrangements, required a wall tablet to protect the wall from plant material. The tablets or *kakeita* were about forty-seven inches long and tapered from five inches at the base to a little more than two inches at the top. A long slot with a clamp, for varying the height of the peg from which a container hung, was part of the device.

Gourds and baskets for hanging arrangements

Clearly gourds and baskets were suitably light-weight containers for hanging arrangements, but sometimes ancient pots and bottles were used for the *kakebana*.

Early pottery

Primitive Japanese pottery of the proto-historic period, and known as *jomon-doki* earthenware, is very highly esteemed by the Japanese Flower Masters. I have never aspired to possess such a piece but have an equally

155 Variation 4 *risshin kei*. The Peruvian
gourd (decorated with a design of llamas
by a red hot wire) makes a suitable
container if used with a *well-kenzan* inside it.

ancient bottle, acquired in Peru, from the grave of some pre-Inca fisher-
man in the desert north of Lima. The patina is quite earthen from the
original firing and centuries buried in dry sand. The decoration is raised
and consists of 'pimples' enclosed by a circle and the semblance of a pre-
historic quadruped with a spinal serration but which I think is a chame-
leon. My Peruvian 'stirrup-pots' having the semblance of birds and animals are known as 'huacos'. In these the *chicha* (Inca home-brewed beer)

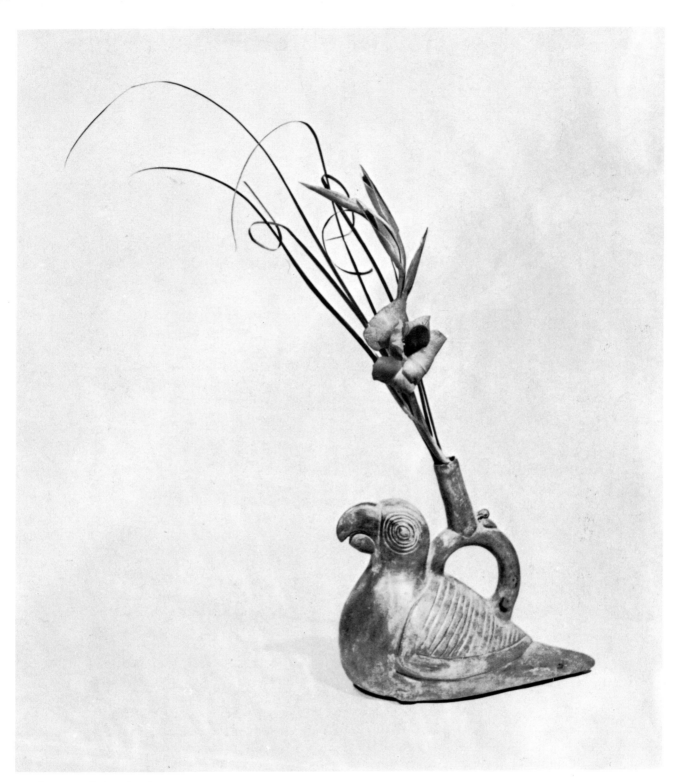

156 These animalistic and ancient pre-Columbian stirrup pots from Peru are called 'huacos' and make interesting flower containers. In this parrot-shaped pot scarlet gladiolus and pampas grass are used.

was served; they do not suggest *jomon-doki* but are invaluable for a fantasy arrangement evoking thoughts of forgotten civilisation. I permit myself the licence of using these pots for Ikebana because I believe that ethnologically the Japanese, Mayan and pre-Inca civilisations derived from a common stock, but the Japanese mingled with the Malaysian race and it is from them that they have surely acquired their love of beauty and perfection in art.

157 A small five-material *seika* type arrangement using young palm, foxtails, bleached fern, astilbe and peonies in a Japanese ceramic standing on a *kwadai*.

158 OPPOSITE ABOVE: *Tsuri fune* or 'boat under way'. A hanging arrangement of an antique bronze boat with flowering currant for *shin* (the sail), and *hikae* (the steering scull); clivia is used for *soe*.

159 OPPOSITE BELOW: A *moribana* arrangement of willow and roses, in a Japanese ceramic, shows how branches can be bent to give movement recalling the Japanese saying: The willows paint the wind.

The leading schools of Ikebana

In Japan there are twenty-three leading schools with a large following of instructors, and in two schools alone there are over one hundred thousand teachers and a million pupils. It is estimated that there are some two to three thousand schools altogether.

Ikebana is considered a vital part of the training for girls, and as it embraces art, calligraphy, philosophy and history, it is a valuable addition to the curriculum for feminine education.

According to the 1967 Directory of Ikebana International (the world-wide cultural and non-profit-making Association), those schools with accredited teachers living outside Japan are:

Chiko School	*Kofu School	Ryusei-Ha
En-Shofu School	Koryu Katabami-Kai	Saga School
*Enshu School	Koryu Shogetsu-Kai	Seifu Enshu-Ryu
Gekka Soami School	Koryu Shoto-Kai	Senke School
*Ichiyo Academy of	Misho-Ryu Bunpo-Kai	Shofu School
Floral Art	Misho-Ryu (Hihara)	*Sogetsu School
*Ikenobo Institute	Nisshin Ryu	Soshin Jikuka School
Kazen School	*Ohara School	*Wafu-Kai

(Those shown with an asterisk are the seven leading schools.)

Why is this vigorous and progressive art favoured with such a vast following, not only in Japan but overseas? I believe the answer is because of the two-fold benefit it brings.

First, there is a great satisfaction and spiritual exaltation in doing Ikebana. This satisfaction is much greater than the mere decorative value of an arrangement. Secondly, its practice makes us much more composed people — a valuable achievement in a tense world.

Progress in not rapid. Advancement in all schools is a slow progress, from one certificate of proficiency to another, and then from diploma to teacher's diploma. As a rule, courses take four to five years, but one never stops learning. I must add that, from my own experience, one only begins to understand Ikebana fully when one teaches it. The realisation that this is the true beginning does not come until then.

Most of the schools in Japan have a Teachers' Association which is like a Trade or Craft Guild. For modest annual dues the members all over the world receive from their Flower Master illustrated details of trends and development at source, together with reports on Tokyo exhibitions, of which there is at least one a month.

Since there is not any competition in these exhibitions, the people attending are the judges of merit. Pupils of a given school flock to see what

the Master has created that is new. In the vast concourse of spectators, those wishing to learn the art decide, after comparing exhibitions, what school to follow.

It must be stated clearly that all schools derive from the same fountainhead of rules and philosophies which were the secrets of the Masters for centuries. The Ikenobo School is five-hundred years old and is the ancestor of them all. Broadly speaking, all schools base their teaching on the principles of plant growth. If one looks at a tree when it is bared of its leaves, the growth principle is very clear and easily understood. Referring to *plate 188*, one perceives that the top section grows upright suggesting upright styles with main stems not more than fifteen degrees from the vertical. The centre section shows how the branches grow slanting suggesting slanting styles. They are slightly curved and vary from fifteen to ninety degrees off the vertical. The bottom section shows how the branches grow hanging, suggesting the hanging or cascading styles as the branches are more than ninety degrees off the vertical. They are generally curved and the tips turn up toward the sun.

The *shoka* or *seika* classical style is derived from these lines as shown in *plate 188*. This also shows why the *seika* style must have its stems close together as though one growth, and at the same time be devoid of any foliage for it represents the trunk of the tree. One is taught that this clearance should be the distance of two hands breadth, which is six to eight inches.

From the *seika* style the *moribana* was created by Unshin Ohara, who cut off the part below the line between A and B (*plate 188*).

The choice of school depends on the individual. Those who favour the austerity of traditional Ikebana will choose the Ikenobo School, which was established in 1500, and the present *Iemoto*, or Headmaster, Mr. Senei Ikenobo, is of the forty-fifth generation of teachers. There are Ikenobo Institutes in both Tokyo and Kyoto. Modern tuition comprises *nageire*, naturalistic *moribana*, *shoka* or *seika* (formal, ancient and modern), and *jiyubana* or free style. The courses take approximately two and a half years for one to reach the grade of Instructor and thereafter one year for each grade of advancement.

An off-shoot of the Ikenobo School which is much favoured is the Koryu School. This was originated by the late Rifuku Enomoto, who was greatly esteemed as a Flower Master and teacher. The *seika*, which derives from the Edo era when Ikebana was adopted by the common people as a simplification of the splendid *rikka* (*plates 162-3*), developed on the stage

161 ABOVE: A Koryu type arrangement of broom, with a few foxtails for *tome* instead of small flowers, in the five-stem *honde ike seika* style. The nineteenth century bronze *usubata* stands on a *kwadai*.

160 OPPOSITE: Free style grevillea and gladiolus arrangement suggests an animal sheltering beneath a tree.

162 and 163 BELOW: Components of a 9-branch classical *rikka* (formal upright style). 4 is upright; 1, 7 and 2 go to north west; 3 and 5 go to north east; 8 goes to south east; 6 and 9 go to south or front.

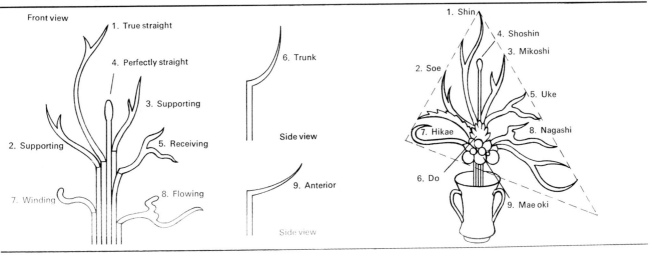

Front view
1. True straight
4. Perfectly straight
3. Supporting
5. Receiving
2. Supporting
7. Winding
8. Flowing

6. Trunk
Side view
9. Anterior
Side view

1. Shin
4. Shoshin
3. Mikoshi
2. Soe
5. Uke
7. Hikae
8. Nagashi
6. Do
9. Mae oki

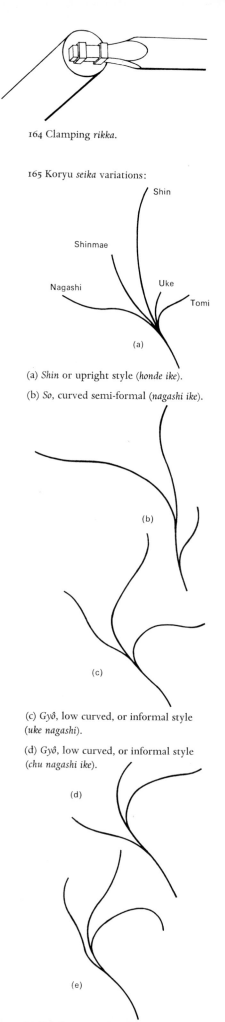

164 Clamping *rikka*.

165 Koryu *seika* variations:

Shin

Shinmae

Nagashi

Uke

Tomi

(a)

(a) *Shin* or upright style (*honde ike*).

(b) *So*, curved semi-formal (*nagashi ike*).

(b)

(c)

(c) *Gyô*, low curved, or informal style (*uke nagashi*).

(d) *Gyô*, low curved, or informal style (*chu nagashi ike*).

(d)

(e)

(e) *Gyô*, low curved style (*tomi nagashi ike*).

of the *tokonoma* and became the classic Japanese style of arranging flowers. The Koryu *seika* had the three main stems of heaven, man and earth but with a different nomenclature. Heaven was *shin*, but earth was called *uke*, meaning 'to receive', and man was called *nagashi* signifying 'to flow'. Supplementary branches were *shinmae* and *tome* — making five in all, from which the style *honde ike* was evolved as the basic style (see *plates 165* and *186*). In this style, and the variations of it, measurements were precise. The three types of *seika* are included in the variations. *Shin* is the upright and formal, almost straight main line style known in *rikka* as *shin* style. The second and third variations are termed *gyô*, expressing semi-formal or moderate curved movement, and *sô* which has very curved movement and is a wide arrangement in informal style.

All these can be done with evergreen material only, but they look more beautiful when the fifth element is flowers. The flowers nestle between the tall *shin* line and the short line of *uke*, and are said to be 'in the valley'.

It is permissible to use a *kenzan* to place the branches but the classic method was a metal ring of substantial weight and a forked *kubari* twig.

The Sogetsu School is favoured by those who prefer less rigid rules for creative art. Tuition comprises naturalistic *moribana*, *nageire* and *jiyubana* (free) styles. Certificates are granted according to the ability of the student and consequently no definite time is set. Mr. Sofu Teshigahara, the Headmaster, aims at freedom of expression, while conforming to traditional philosophies. It is also the aim of this school to promote better human relationships through love of flower arranging.

The Ohara School, directed by the grandson of the founder Unshin Ohara, Mr. Houn Ohara, has centres in Tokyo and Kobe. This school was founded at the end of the nineteenth century, when it modernised Ikebana by the introduction of *moribana*, or low bowl naturalistic arrangements. This popular school will be favoured by those who prefer rather full types of arrangement which are well suited to Western homes.

The Ohara School has two basic styles, *moribana* low bowl and *heika* (or *nageire*) tall vase. Each of these has five variations:
1. Upright style.
2. Slanting style, including 'water-reflecting style'.

167 The boats in classical Japanese arrangements were usually of bamboo, while the older ones from China were of ceramic. In the 19th century bronze ones were used. The boat in the photograph is of darkened nickel, made by the silversmith Michael Murray to the author's design. It has a false perspective effect at the stern and a graceful high prow. The upright irises in *seika* style suggest a 'boat at anchor', with furled sails, called *tomari fune*.

166 LEFT: Free style arrangement of clivia and daffodil leaves with a megasea leaf for *hikae*. Stones hide the *kenzan* in this deep blue Japanese ceramic. The emphasis is on colour harmony.

168 RIGHT: Young palm, delphinium in light and dark blue shades with Summer grasses are used to illustrate a design of straight lines crossed by curved ones. The bowl is of hammered copper with silver appliqué Inca motifs of aquatic birds round the rim and was made by the Peruvian artist Laffi.

169 EXTREME RIGHT: In the dark blue *suiban* fragrant mimosa is used for *shin* and *soe*, while *hikae* is a yellow double tulip supported by two *jushis*. It should be noted that the shape of this basic *risshin kei* is enclosed by a scalene triangle.

171 A Japanese frog-shaped ceramic
flower holder. The heavy metal ring
protects bowls from damage when
using fixture techniques. A forked
twig *kubari* holder is wedged in the
ring, not against the container.
The bottom picture shows the metal
ring used with the *kubari* (fork) and
wedging *ichimongi* (bar). Used for
Koryu School *seika* in a medium
bowl which hides the ring fixture.

170 OPPOSITE ABOVE: In this *heishin kei* arrangement the *shin* of pussy-willow is placed low and just above the rim of the celadon dish. Supplementary stems follow the same line: *hikae* similarly being the same material. *Soe* is a flower in this variation with supporting *jushis* of pink tulips. *Tomi* is of berberis buds and a few river pebbles.

172 LEFT: The Ichiyo School teaches that the enclosing shape of a scalene triangle is generally successful. In this free style arrangement of bunched violets, curling vines and megasea leaves the principle is clearly shown.

173 ABOVE: A modern arrangement of marguerites and bronze-hued berberis leaves in a mottled blue glaze Japanese container having openings at two levels. The design is by Meikof Kasuya, Headmaster of the Ichiyo School. The arrangement is based on the concept of *in* and *yo* or complementary elements.

174 ABOVE RIGHT: The *risshin kei* basic upright arrangement of bunched gladioli for shin and supporters with bleached broom for *soe* and *hikae* in an Egyptian copper bowl again illustrates the principle of a scalene triangle enclosing shape.

3. Cascade style, or 'cliff overhanging', drooping and falling style.
4. Heavenly style, tall and upright.
5. Contrasting style, emphasising the contrast between flowers and foliage, or contrast between the lines of the main stem and those of the flowers.

In addition, the Ohara School teaches modern arrangements in the following free style manner:

Realistic: *Scenic trend*, creating a miniature landscape in a bowl.
Colour trend, emphasising lovely colour harmonies; most suited to *heika* style.

Non-Realistic: *Image trend*, using strange and unusual materials regardless of the way they grow.
Shape trend, using natural materials for the sake of their colour and shape. Flowers are used for colour mass and shape. In this harmony and contrast of colour are associated with texture and movement.

Formative: No vase is required and all types of material are used. It is usually sculptural and monumental.
Abstract trend, with basic emphasis on colour and form
Vision trend is a surrealistic expression based on a mental picture.

The Ohara School has a very large following, its Headmaster having travelled widely. It is considered of equal rating with the Sogetsu School.

All schools, it is seen, teach *moribana* low bowl and *nageire* tall vase style arrangements. The merit of the Ichiyo Academy of Floral Art is in its simplified system of tuition. The four courses for a teacher's certificate

175 *Niju kiri* arrangement with cherry blossom and white iris.

176 RIGHT: An ancient unglazed bottle-shaped pot from Peru, probably of pre-Inca origin, is cherished for its craftsmanship as well as its antiquity because it has the quality of *shibui*. It is here shown as it might be used for *chabana* as a simple hanging arrangement.

can be telescoped into one hundred hours over one year, but it is better to extend it to two years of study. The Academy conducts a correspondence course from Tokyo and has a Master covering all Europe as representative. Founded in 1937, this progressive school is directed by Meikof Kasuya. Tuition includes *jiyubana* (free) styles closely related to the principles of the basic styles. It is ideal for those with limited time, due to pressures of work and household, and for this reason is gaining worldwide appreciation.

Another school gaining in size is the Wafu-Kai directed by Mr. Wafu Teshigahara. The school was founded in 1907, and tuition comprises naturalistic *moribana* and *nageire*. Courses take approximately two years and, after gaining proficiency and passing an examination, a teacher's diploma can be obtained. Mr. Wafu is a popular teacher who also conducts correspondence courses.

Detailed information regarding the various schools and lists of teachers' addresses throughout the world can be obtained from the Publication Department, Ikebana International, GPO Box 1262, Tokyo, Japan. The annual world-wide Directory of Teachers is also available from this

177 This bulbous gourd, sometimes called a calabash, reveals the source of inspiration which led many oriental potters to copy its graceful form. The shape is well suited for either a wall hanging or a standing arrangement. The pale flowers of Nelly Moser clematis are chosen because they would contrast with the sombre tones of the surroundings if this arrangement were used as a *chabana* in the Tea House.

178 RIGHT: A lily in an upright arrangement using a wave-form container made by the author for Meikof Kasuya.

address at the cost of $ US 1.25 per copy.

With the growing popularity of Ikebana, there will undoubtedly, before long, be teachers of all the important schools in most countries. More and more people find solace and relief from tension in this creative art and become qualified to help others. It should be stressed that it is an art which cannot be learned from a book alone. The criticism and watchful guidance of a tutor is essential. Even after the successful conclusion of correspondence courses it is advisable to study with a Master so that faults may be corrected.

Ikebana is especially helpful to the housebound, the aged and the sick who must temporarily be immobilised. It possesses a therapeutic value which is becoming recognised more and more. At any age, the challenge to master the mechanical and artistic problems of Ikebana provides spiritual satisfaction — always provided time is not unduly limited.

It does not matter which school is followed since all roads lead to beauty and composure of spirit. The important thing is to select a school for its teaching methods rather than its trend. While the nomenclature of stems and flowers differs for all schools, the basic principles are the same.

129

7 What about the flowers?

179 *Seika* arrangement of reconstituted narcissi in a white porcelain sugar basin.

Using cut blooms

I have not forgotten the flowers. I have said earlier that they are of secondary importance, in order to stress the prior claim on our attention of the setting in which the flowers, like a gem, will be placed. They are also the manifestation of the ultimate beauty on earth and, because this beauty is unfortunately so transitory, we have to use every possible method to lengthen their lives. For this, we draw largely on what used to be the secrets of the ancient schools in Japan — but this knowledge is now freely available.

Preservation of flowers

All cut plants wilt sooner or later despite the greatest care. The process of transpiration whereby 'aliveness' or freshness is maintained by water or the plant's life-giving sap, depends on the conditions in which the cuttings are placed, as well as gentle treatment. Evaporation from the petals varies in degree, according to the species, as well as the capacity of the stems to permit water-rising.

Two matters therefore concern us. First, the climate or atmosphere in which the flowers are placed must be considered. Ideally it should be humid, of low temperature and free from strong light and warmth as well as draughts. Like people, flowers can be hardened by exposure to cold, provided they are sheltered from wind and protected from frost. Humidity can be provided artificially by atomising moisture from a spray at regular intervals.

The water-rising, which the Japanese call *mizuage*, can be augmented by measures determined by the classification of the cutting. For instance, flowers such as violets react best to total immersion in cold water at frequent intervals. This prevents the rate of transpiration from the petals exceeding the rate of water rising through the thread-like stems. To preserve and harden, seal in a polythene bag, after shaking off surplus water, and place in the refrigerator but as far as possible from the freezing compartment.

Secondly, wilting of cut material is hastened by lack of moisture in the tissues because of air in the water ducts of stems and also from slime and bacteria on the cut surfaces. Whenever a stem is cut, atmospheric pressure forces air into the ducts where there is normally a partial vacuum. The airlocks so caused impede water-rising when the stem is put in water, and the remedy is to cut long-stemmed flowers and sprays of foliage *under water*. This is a golden rule in arranging and is exceedingly important.

After cutting from the parent stem of plants, preservation can be effected by holding the cut ends for two minutes in boiling water. Care should be taken to protect the cut flowers of foliage from heat and steam by wrapping it in a damp towel. An alternative method is to char one inch off the end. Cuttings should then be placed in the deep water of a full bucket for one or two hours prior to arranging.

It should be mentioned here that a very sharp knife is less injurious to the cells and ducts of stems than the pinching action of secateurs and scissors. The Japanese *hasami*, flower scissors, are however designed to minimise this pinching action.

Slime formation can be minimised by a quick dip in rubbing alcohol when placement is made. This is obtainable from a chemist, and the stems should be dipped in it for two or three seconds only. Some arrangers use a diluted solution of acetic acid, which is also obtainable from a chemist. Stimulant solutions are also used for soft-fibred cuttings and the stems of acquatic plants, the latter often being applied by injection, using a small pump.

Broadly, we can say that woody cuttings, such as chrysanthemums and roses should be treated with hot water or charring. Plants which exude milky sap, like dahlias, hollyhock and poppy, should be seared to seal the ends and keep the life-giving sap inside. Succulent plants, such as arum lilies and water lilies and also spring bulb flowers, must be stood upright in deep water for at least an hour, pumping water into them before arranging if possible.

Stems of narcissi, to be used for *seika* arrangements, should be chosen for the buds rather than the opened flowers. If there are too many open flowers, all but two or three should be removed. Three stems only are required, and these should be laid flat and 'ironed' toward the cut end with the handle of the scissors. This is done to squeeze out all the slimy sap. Then, taking four leaves of different lengths, two leaves are placed on each side of the stem so that the insides of the leaves are toward the stem. The three composite stems are then loosely bound with cotton, to keep the five elements of each together, and floral gutta percha tape is wound round the bottom end to simulate the sheath in which the flowers grow naturally. The re-composition of each flower and leaves is to thin out the natural growth. If it is found possible to use the sheath which has had to be removed it is certainly better to do so, but it is a skilled operation and not for beginners, until they have been shown by a teacher.

After preparation, the three re-composed stems should be plunged into cold and deep water which will rise in place of the removed sap.

A little salt is sometimes used to arrest wilting, particularly of bamboo, the leaves of which quickly start drying and rolling after cutting from the parent stem. I have found that the pressing of bamboo leaves with a cool iron dries them out flatly so that they retain their original feathery beauty. The leaves can then be bent into natural curves by stroking them between the fingers. This pressing technique can also be applied to brilliantly coloured leaves when they start turning colour in autumn. They should be picked for this before they are too dry and ready to drop.

There are many proprietary stimulant preparations marketed for plants, but I recommend all students to experiment on the bases outlined above in order to become acquainted with the most practical and the simplest methods of preservation for each classification of material. The understanding of what causes wilting prematurely helps the study of methods to check it, whereas making up and following intricate, and sometimes special, formulae might be considered out of place in our busy world. Without visual proof of effectiveness, many may remain uncon-

vinced. To them, I suggest taking two identical plant cuttings, treating one and doing nothing to the other. Place them in jars of water close to each other and so compare the results of treatment.

Dealing with your florist
Flower arrangers who have gardens usually grow for their requirements. They are able to choose, cut and condition their material with a minimum of problems, providing they cut during the cool of early morning or evening. Those without gardens must obtain their material from a florist, and they should find a reliable one with a view to continued custom and his understanding of special requirements. Usually the larger the firm and the bigger the turnover, the more understanding one receives. I have found that when a supplier knows that one is practising floral art

he is usually very helpful, often supplying the names of special varieties and also giving hints on durability and origin.

When buying, choose flowers with care. They should preferably be in bud and the foliage should be crisp, not drooping. Examine petals carefully for the faintest sign of crinkly effect, which indicates the onset of wilting. Avoid such blooms.

For those without gardens, there are also potted plants from which neither branches nor flowers may be drawn but the odd leaf can be used. These people have the best of both worlds in some ways, avoiding the labour and expense of a garden, yet having exotics around them when the gardens outside look miserable in the bad season. A Begonia Rex leaf or one from a monstera plant, with a couple of exotic flowers from the florist, can look lovely as well as being unusual.

Growing shrubs for arranging

The Director of one of the world's biggest floral art concerns once confided in me that he never grew flowers — except uncommon little alpines — and he concentrated on his garden of shrubs because these could not be bought at the market for stems in flower arranging. He also saw to it that his chosen shrubs for arranging were especially favoured with careful study of the soil and sunshine, necessitating the trial of different positions.

In Ikebana one uses what is available, despising no humble plant life that is indigenous. Thus in each region there is developing a type of Ikebana suited to the climate, and perhaps in the foreseeable future we may look forward to an Olympic type of Flower Festival honouring the different countries throughout the world.

Drying and preservation of flowers

In temperate zones, where the winters necessitate central heating, one turns to dried materials for winter use. It is not necessary to buy vividly-dyed dried materials. It is much more fun to dry them oneself and keep them stored in boxes. Far preferable are the natural hues of beige and brown, mahogany and flame, when mixed with soft blues and purples of delphiniums and immortelles. Suitable storage space is essential as boxes of dried material should be disturbed as little as possible. Most material is dried hanging upside-down in bunches.

The glycerine process is well known, and it is only necessary here to remind one that standing branches in a mixture of equal parts of cheap glycerine and hot water and leaving them for two or three weeks will ensure having leafy branches throughout the winter. (Anti-freeze can also be used for this mixed with double the quantity of water.)

Fragile flowers are usually dried in boxes, covered lightly with a mixture of borax, or alum, and cornmeal. They should be processed only when perfectly dry, laid on the mixture and lightly sprinkled with some of it. Three or four days is sufficient, as a rule. Another drying process is that of pressing between sheets of newspaper under a carpet. In two or three weeks the leaves will have dried out, retaining a flat shape. One must cut such material before the sap has started to run back for best results. Part of the drying process is ironing dampened leaves when they start to curl. Young acacia seed pods respond to this treatment and preserve their cherry colour. Bamboo also responds, and this is a boon for exhibitions because the leaves start to curl into rolls almost as soon as the stems are cut. A cool iron will preserve the vivid green and keep the leaves flat. They can be curved by stroking between the fingers after arranging.

133

8 How did it all begin?

181 Picture of the facsimile fresco of lilies and griffins in the Throne Room of the Palace of Knossus, Crête, circa 1500 B.C.

The art of flower arrangement is as ancient as painting and sculpture. Garlands of lotus and other blooms, found placed as offerings on mummy cases, indicate that there were floral artists in the time of the Pharaohs.

A love of flowers, and indeed of all nature, is also shown in the Minoan frescoes which adorned the Palace of Knossus and the villas at Haghia Triada and Amnissos in Crête, excavated by Sir Arthur Evans early this century. In a facsimile of this art of the second millenium BC, we see today the designs of tall lilies, iris, crocus, herbs and grasses swaying in the breeze as well as the first rose in graphic art. This leaves no doubt whatever that this ancient people loved nature intensely.

So from Egypt, Asia Minor and Crête religious rites and fertility cults came to the mainland of Greece. The mythical story of the abduction of Persephone, earth-mother Demeter's daughter, by King Pluto of the underworld, and her annual return with the Spring flowers, symbolises, of course, the cycle of the seasons.

Pagan floral rites passed from Greece to Rome, and either the Romans or earlier Phoenicians from Asia Minor brought them to Britain and Gaul. The 'corn dolly' made in rural England is still found today in villages of the Peloponnese. This skilfully plaited figure, with a tassel of bearded ears, is thought to be a votive offering to the fertility earth-goddess, who bestowed the gift of agricultural knowledge on Prince Triptolemus as a reward for his help in Demeter's search for her daughter.

In Derbyshire we have yet another beautiful flower custom. At several villages, such as Ewell and Tissington, the villagers make floral pictures

182 Votive offerings of Lotus on altar of Buddha, showing right hand and left hand arrangements according to the side of the statue on which they are placed.

183 A landscape scroll painting.

184 A 'semi-formal' *rikka*.

to 'dress the well' and honour the precious source of their water.

Flower arranging in South East Asian countries seems originally to have been mainly concerned with the lotus. We learn that cuttings of this lovely flower symbolised beauty and purity of spirit, rising heavenward from the mud of pools — the mundane things of life. Moreover the lotus was arranged, especially in India and China, as a votive offering to Great Buddha, reflecting All Time — the Past of the seed pod, the Present of the flower and the Future of the unfurled leaf and bud.

Professor Minobu Ohi, of the Institute of History of Japan, in her profound study of the history of Ikebana, believes that its origin is to be found in *kuge* — the custom of floral offerings to Buddha, which became prevalent at temples in the sixth century. The lotus was arranged in a basket or bowl, and even bronze artificial flowers called *renchi* were used. In the oldest chronicles of Japan — the *Nihon Shoki* — it is recorded that 'every plant can well express itself'. The same thought is behind the art of Ikebana today. We teach how the flowers can indicate to the arranger the best way to arrange them, and we point out this symbolism of the life-force which is short-lived in certain plants but enduring in evergreens such as pine which is therefore used on festive occasions.

Flower arranging in Japan

Buddhism came to Japan from China, via Korea, early in the sixth century. A fervent Buddhist and reformer, Shotoku Taishi, prince and son of the Emperor Yomei, is believed to have originated flower arrangement in Japan. A great scholar, he promulgated a code of laws as well as introducing the Chinese calendar. During his regency, cultural exchanges with China were started. Temples became schools of doctrine, faith and wisdom. Classics, calligraphy, painting and the arts were taught because of their civilising influences. So it came about that an ambassador named Ono no Imoko, of royal descent, was sent three times to China. Ono no Imoko ultimately became the guardian of a temple in Kyoto for the worship of Nyoi-Rin-Kwannon, the omnipowerful Buddhist divinity of love. Ono no Imoko occupied a priest's dwelling close to a pool in the temple gardens. The dwelling was referred to as *ike no bo* — 'the hut near the pond' — and according to tradition the first arrangements of flowers were made there.

Ono no Imoko adopted the name of Senmo. His long line of descendants, continuing his school, which is known today as the Ikenobo School, all include the syllable of 'sen' in their names.

The fundamental rules and principles of the Ikenobo School were established by the twelfth holder of the title — Senkei — who was a great nature lover and travelled widely seeking rare plant specimens. He brought the complex *rikka* style — a huge floral composition suggesting a beautiful landscape — to a high degree of perfection before he died in 1028. Senjun, the twenty-sixth Headmaster, was born in 1417 when Japan was at the height of her power under the Ashikaga Shoguns. The *dobushus*, or retainers of court noblemen, were adept in the art of arranging *rikkas* for their patrons, but in the time of Yohsimasha (1443-1472), who took a great interest in all art, the teaching of flower arranging reverted to the Ikenobo Masters. Yoshimasha decreed that Masters of the Ikenobo School should become known as *Iemoto* — 'Originator of the Art of Flower Arrangement', a title pertaining strictly to the head priest of the Rokkaku Temple in Kyoto.

Rikka arrangements, often being man-high and too large for ordinary

185 Corn 'dollies' from Corinth.

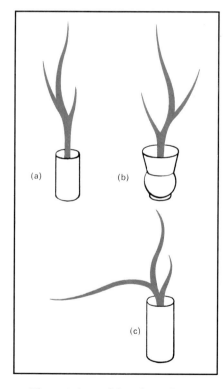

186 The main lines of three-line *seikas* are (a) the 'formal' style right hand arrangement, (b) the 'semi-formal' style left hand arrangement, and (c) the 'informal' style right hand arrangement.

homes, Senjun evolved a new and simpler form called *nageire*, drew up rules and wrote treatises. This in turn became later simplified and was known as *seika* or *shoka*. These simpler arrangements led to the evolution of the alcove, or *tokanoma*, a place of honour to display an arrangement, usually with a painted scroll, called a *kakemono*.

The informal *nageire* style (meaning 'thrown in') was sometimes known as *chabana*, or tea ceremony arrangement. This was because of its associations with the tea ceremony, *chanoyu*, founded by Sen No Rikyo, in the sixteenth century. He asserted that the ceremony is in essence simplicity, bringing comfort and spiritual joy to all humanity. It followed that for *chabana*, the flowers and vase must be as simple as possible, in keeping with the ceremony. Often a bamboo container and a single bloom — of light colour to contrast with the tea utensils — were composed in elegant simplicity. The arrangement, however, evoked thoughts of a beautiful garden. This concept is conveyed by the Japanese word, characterising their best art: it is *shibui* or refined simplicity.

The *rikka* style continued to enjoy great popularity, being appropriate for decorating the castles of feudal lords, who, together with their retainers, practised the art. In general, they practised a style called *sunamono*, which means a semi-informal style, not too upright but slightly curved, yet not as curved as the *sunabachi* style, which evolved from it. The *sunabachi* was a low bronze bowl with a tray for sand resting on the inside rim like a lid and which served to cover the placement of material. The name derives from *suna*, meaning sand, which was used symbolically to suggest a landscape. *Sunabachi* are ornate bronze pieces rarely found today. They came originally from China and were embellished with animal and vegetable motifs and often bore inscriptions.

A treatise written in 1545, the *Ikenobo-sen'ei densho*, laid down the names, proportions and placements of the seven principal branches for *rikka*. This is enlightening, as it gives a clue to the artist's thoughts behind the composition. The seven branches (*plates 162-3*) are:

Shin: the true straight branch, standing in the centre and suggesting a high mountain. It also suggests the feudal lord ruling his land.

Soe: the supporting branch, suggesting a distant mountain.

Mikoshi: the supporting branch between *soe* and *uke*.

Shoshin: the straight up branch, suggesting a central peak.

Uke: the 'receiving branch', suggesting the closest mountain.

Nagashi: the 'flowing branch', suggesting a near road.

Mae oki: the 'anterior branch', the body of the arrangement suggesting near mountains.

Thus each branch signified the component of a landscape. The microcosmos idea was also associated with the principles of *in* and *yo*.

We observe that in the *rikka* arrangement, perspective as we know it does not matter. This is because only a suggestion is made, leaving the viewer to exercise his imagination. Subsequently the *rikka* style had other branches added, making nine branches in all by the time of Ikenobo Master Senjo (1786-1832). The addition of branches called *hikae* and *do* made up the 'nine branched *rikka*' of the eighteenth century.

In this way, and with continued Imperial patronage, the early Masters evolved an art form which had an educational role in the lives of the people. It taught people to ponder on the designs of nature, manifested in all plant material when deftly arranged, and in which there was the deep spiritual significance to which allusion is made above.

It should be recalled that Japan was essentially a man's world, and until

136

1868 Ikebana was generally practised only by men.

The development of *seika* started in the eighteenth century. This style combined the dignity of the *rikka* with the informal simplicity of *nageire*. Many schools of *seika* style became established, some of them still in existence today. The *seika* became more simplified with increased popularity until, in the early nineteenth century, the design became broadly based on a scalene triangle. The asymmetric beauty of thus enclosing the area for the design clearly follows nature's laws of tree and leaf growth.

In the *seika* we see very clearly the evolution of the popular flower arrangement, the three principal branches symbolising heaven, man and earth, which are easily arranged and within the scope of everybody (see *plate 186*). The *seika* also reflected the taste of rich and powerful merchants, who vied with each other in the magnificence of their containers, rather than in the excellence of their arrangements. Painted scrolls of the Meija era, 1868, show that women were learning the new formalised art as an accomplishment because the simplicity of the *seika* so perfectly suited room decoration. There was also a trend to abandon traditional customs in favour of novelties. The ancient schools, however, continued their teaching and ignored Western ideas which, with increased commercial exchanges, had begun to infiltrate Japan. Western style flower arrangement, which was called *yo bana*, offended their restrained taste. Paradoxically, they had for centuries acted on the same precept as that of Cleobulus — one of the Seven Sages of ancient Greece — who in the sixth century BC had propounded 'nothing in excess'.

By 1887 there came the great revival of nationalism in Japan. Ikebana, together with *chanoyu*, again became an aesthetic accomplishment. Whirlpools of vulgar Western taste swept round the unique and isolated rock of Japan's restrained simplicity in her art which became more widespread. Young women had been taught Ikebana in order to become 'good wives and wise mothers', and it had become an indispensable accomplishment, as well as a teaching profession, for women.

By the turn of the century, and resulting from the introduction to Japan of our lovely European flowers, a new trend of flower arrangement steadily gained popularity. Keeping the triad of the three main branches, flower master Unshin Ohara created the *moribana* style — shallow bowl arrangements — and founded his school, Ohara Ryu, in 1897. It is easily seen that by cutting out the part of the *seika* below the point where the three branches cease to appear as one stem, the *nemoto*, down to the water level, we have the basic form for *moribana* style.

The colour and decorative beauty of *moribana* quickly became fashionable, and the disciples of Unshin Ohara came to establish their schools, during the period 1912-1925 (the Taisho Era). They specialised in variations of the new style, many of which were influenced by and reflected European art. This led to 'free style' arrangements, called *jiyubana*.

In 1926 the Showa era began. While in Europe the visual arts were unfettered, with the exploration of new concepts and media, modern ways of living had penetrated Japan. This, together with the influence of 'avant garde' art, brought about the inevitable break with traditional ideas and also brought Ikebana out of the alcove *tokonoma*. Henceforth it would be viewed from three sides instead of only from the front. Creative originality became a more important characteristic of arrangements and led to the introduction of other materials. The pre-requisites now became line or design, depth and colour: viewing from three sides made depth imperative, that is, more filling between back and front. All

187 A well-dressing at Eyam in Derbyshire.

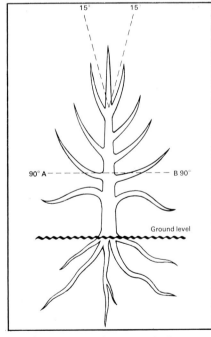

188 The top section shows upright form or style. Branches mostly angles 0° to 15°. Centre section has branches of slanting form. Branches are slightly curved and angles from the vertical axis vary from 15° to 90°. The bottom section shows branches of hanging or cascading form which are more than 90° from the vertical axis. Mostly curved and tips turn up to sun.

189 A well-dressing at Eyam in Derbyshire.

190 Sculptural abstract double arrangement using pots made by the author to illustrate the theme, 'the parched earth'. The foxtails of *shin* suggest clouds, the teased grasses of *soe* represent the rain falling and the *hikae* of buttercups in the small pot indicate the flowers blooming after the rain. The large pot is suggestive of a head with open mouth gasping for water.

sorts of new materials came to be used, including shells, pebbles, driftwood, gnarled roots and weather-worn stones. The Japanese are an artistic and also an impressionable people. They revere and are moved by all manifestations of nature, including imperfections such as dwarfed trees growing in the crack of a rock, strange twisting and contorted material like vines and bare branches with a few blossoms, as found on early prunus. That they follow closely the scenic changes of season is evidenced by the floral patterns of the women's kimonos. The new materials used for Ikebana met the requirements of design to evoke feelings of nostalgia, gaiety or serenity. Even the water in the *moribana* bowl (although it had the practical function of absorbing more oxygen for the life of the flowers) was a part of the design suggesting coolness on a Summer day.

Thus *zen'ei bana* was born, establishing the link between floral art and the plastic arts of the outside world. Foremost in popularising *zen'ei bana* was the Japanese sculptor Sofu Teshigahara. After the Second World War, his artistic creations met the needs of the post-war generation and speedily soared, not only to national but to international popularity. This was largely because they suited Western and Eastern surroundings.

Foremost among foreign teachers who have graduated in Japan are Ellen Gordon Allen, wife of an American General, and Norman J. Sparnon, artist, potter and designer from Australia. Both finding themselves in Tokyo because of the Korean war, they studied Ikebana assiduously. Ellen Allen studied classical *seika* at the Saga School and became a graduate teacher of the Ohara School, of which Houn Ohara, grandson of the founder Unshin, is Headmaster. Norman Sparnon studied the classical styles at the Ikenobo School and modern Ikebana at Sogetsu School.

Ellen Allen evolved the idea of creating a world-wide cultural association — Ikebana International — which was founded in Tokyo in August 1956. Its purpose was to stimulate and cultivate the study of Ikebana — all schools — throughout the world. The organisation draws Masters, teachers and students into close contact and, through its publications, keeps them informed of trends and developments in Japan.

Since 1959 the Headmasters of the principal Tokyo schools have made regular tours of the world demonstrating and teaching, and at frequent intervals study groups are organised to visit Japan. The number of teachers accredited and holding Diplomas from their chosen schools in Japan grows steadily larger.

So keen is the enthusiasm to learn the secrets of this ancient art that three major schools in Tokyo have published their manuals for beginners, in English, for the guidance of students all over the world. However, it was Mr. Meikof Kasuya, a former graduate of Sogetsu Ryu, who by founding his Ichiyo School introduced a simplified and highly practical method of teaching. It is based on the way that plants grow and their resultant suitability for various designs.

The meaning of Ikebana is 'living flowers' but it is clear that a more accurate interpretation would be an 'arrangement of plant material'. It does not pretend to represent growing plants, although it may suggest this. Nor is it just a pleasing decoration. It conveys simply an interpretation of nature by a pleasing design. It should never be forgotten it derives from a traditional art embracing symbolism and philosophy. Ikebana is also the study of nature and art blended into harmony in daily living.

Let us then accept graciously this gift from Japan, just as we have accepted the 'cup of humanity' which quenches our thirst and lifts up our spirits at tea time.

Glossary

Aki no nanasaka The seven autumnal flowers: Kudzu vine, Chinese bell-flower, thoroughwort, patrinia, pink, pampas grass (miscanthus) and bush clover.

Ashirai Another name for supporting stems or *jushi*.

Bonkei Landscape in a tray. Usually made of clay.

Bonsai Dwarf trees in a pot.

Bonseki Miniature stone and sand landscape on lacquer board or tray.

Cha Tea. *Cha* is used in composite words to indicate items associated with the Tea Ceremony, such as *cha jin* or tea master. *Chashitsu* or *chasenke* means tea house, *chawan* is tea bowl, *chasen* is the whisk made of bamboo and used to whisk tea in the tea ritual.

Chabana Very simple arrangement for the Tea Ceremony.

Chanoyu The Tea Ceremony.

Dai Stand or base for arrangements.

Defune Outward-bound ship or boat.

Dôwa kubari Metal ring for protection of vase used for holding branches together in arrangements such as Koryu.

Do Front mountain, a component which suggests a hill in the foreground in *rikka* arrangements.

Fune Boat.

Gomi Tray or receptacle for waste material.

Gyô Semi-formal arrangement, slightly curved. (See also *shin* and *sô*.)

Gyô dô ike 'Fish-path' between pebbles in *kabu waki*, Sogetsu fifth variation arrangement.

Hakumi The art of re-grouping flowers, for instance narcissi and leaves in groups for *seika* style.

Haiku The style of brief poetry used to evoke the idea or subject supplying a detail and leaving the reader to develop the idea in his own imagination.

Ha mono Plants with leaves suited for Ikebana.

Hana All plant life and rocks, stones, sand and wood suggesting the cosmic concept.

Hasami Flower and branch-cutting scissors.

Hasu no hana Lotus.

Heika Standing upright style of *nageire* – used in Ohara School.

Heishin kei Sogetsu flat or horizontal style.

Hikae Third main stem in Sogetsu arrangements, representing earth.

Hinamatsuri The Girl's Festival.

Higatte Left hand arrangement, or 'inversed form' which was placed as a votive offering by the statue of Buddha.

Honde ike The formal or *shin* style arrangement, which is the first of the five Koryu School styles of *seika*, the others being *nagashi ike*, the semi-formal style, and the three informal styles *uke nagashi ike*, *chu nagashi ike*, and *tome nagashi ike*.

Hongatte Right hand arrangement, or 'genuine form' placed on the right of a statue of Buddha.

Iemoto Originator of the art of flower arrangement; today a Flower Master (head of a school).

Ikebana Living plant material in water.

Ikenobo The oldest school of Ikebana in Japan.

Imba Leaves with backs toward viewer.

In Chinese *yin* – cloudy. This is the feminine element in philosophical *yin* and *yang* concept. It usually means passive, receiving or earth.

Irefune, or Irebune Homeward-bound boat.

Jiyubana 'Free style' arrangement.

Jushi Supporting branch, flower or leaf.

Kabu wake – stump, *wake* – separate; land and water-plant arrangement, using two *kenzans* as in Sogetsu fifth variation.

Kadai Short-legged stand for arrangements.

Kado The way of flower arranging.

Kago Woven basket.

Kakebana Hanging wall arrangement.

Kakedanaike Wall basket.

Kakeita Long narrow board to protect wall in hanging arrangements.

Kakemono Hanging picture or calligraphic scroll.

Kansui ike Water-viewing arrangements.

Keishin kei Sogetsu School slanting style arrangement.

Kenzan 'Sword mountain' – pinholder.

Kenzan naoshi Small tool, like a clock key, for straightening bent *kenzan* needles.

Kubari Forked (Y-shape) twigs cut to fit vase and hold material firmly in place when using tall vases.

Kwadai Low four-legged table stand for arrangements, sometimes scroll-shaped.

Mae In front of.

Mi mono Berry plants.

Mizuage Preservation of cut material. Water-rising – stimulation of water ducts in plant tissues.

Mizugiri Cutting stems under water to prevent air lock.

Mitsumata Edgeworthia. A popular bleached branch material.

Moribana Arrangement in a low shallow bowl.

Morimono Arrangement of fruit, vegetables or stones sometimes with a few flowers. No water. One of the trio in Sogetsu seventh variation.

Mono Plant.

Nageire Arrangement in a tall vase.

Naki dai Scroll-ended base for classical arrangements.

Nejime Ikenobo School word for focal point or shortest group in an arrangement. Usually of different material from main stems. It is associated with earth grouping and is *in front* of heaven. Seldom used for *shin* and *soe*.

Niju kiri Arrangement in double-tiered container, Ikenobo style.

Nemoto Length of branches from neck of container to the point of division, as in a tree trunk.

Ogencho A temple container, more ancient than the *usubata* and known as a 'black boar' bronze.

Ohina sama The Festival of Dolls.

Oki fune Boat at anchor – motionless.

Ono no imoko The originator of Japanese flower arrangement.

O shogatsu New Year.

Oyo Style.

Rikka or Rikwa Large, ornate Ikenobo arrangement. The oldest style, it means 'standing up plant cuttings'. Intended to suggest a mountain scene. Introduced by Senkei in the late 15th century.

Risshin kei Sogetsu upright style arrangement.

Seika, skoka or skokwa Simplified classical arrangement.

Sensei Teacher.

Shibui Simplicity and refinement.

Shikibana A flat table arrangement of spread flowers without vase. One of the trio of Sogetsu seventh variation.

Shiki-ita A wood or reed base – flat boards.

Shin In traditional arrangements, the 'formal' or fairly straight. In the Sogetsu arrangements the largest main stem (heaven).

Shippo Heavy tubular flower-holder used by Ohara School.

Shogi Translucent standing screen panels.

Sô 'Informal' style in traditional arrangements – very curved.

Soe In Sogetsu arrangements the second largest main stem. Man.

Sogetsu ryu School of the Grass Moon.

Suiban A basin or shallow low bowl.
Suishin kei Hanging style.
Sumie The art of black and white brush painting which originated in China in the sixth century. The black brush strokes had an austere quality of expression especially in calligraphy.
Sunabachi Shallow bronze bowl used for low *rikka* style arrangements with a sand board covering the water.
Tai Ikenobo school term for the third main stem – earth (hikae). Literally material substance.
Tabi Foot mitten sock worn with Japanese sandals.
Tachi zuro A tall bamboo vase cut out to resemble a 'standing crane'.
Taka shoku A tall table on which hanging arrangements are placed.
Tanabata The Star Festival.
Tani Valley with water in classical *rikka* arrangements.
Tatami 6' × 3' straw mats for covering floors.
Tango-no-sekku The Boys' Festival.
Tokonoma The sacred alcove in Japanese homes.
Tomari fune Ship or boat in port, or motionless boat.
Tomi Lowest branch in modern arrangements, or a branch, sometimes quite short material to hide stems of main branches and flower holders.
Tsubo-gata A jar-shaped vase.
Tsuri fune Hanging boat arrangement.
Tsukimo Moon-viewing.
Tsuru mono Vines used in hanging arrangement.
Tsuyo mono Plants weaker than tree plants and stronger than grass plants.
Ukibana Floating flower arrangement, one of the trio of Sogetsu seventh variation.
Ushiro Behind.
Usubata Special container, usually of bronze, for classical arrangements.
Yo The complement of *in*, the positive, male, active, sunny or flowing.
Zen'ei bana 'Avant garde' style.
Zori Japanese sandals.
Zundo A formal vase in a plain tubular type of bamboo.

Bibliography

Ikebana Sogetsu Flower Arrangement Sofu Teshigahara
Sofu: His Boundless World of Flowers and Form Sofu Teshigahara
Space and Colour in Japanese Flower Arrangement Kasumi Teshigahara
Ikebana Ohara School Flower Arrangement Houn Ohara
The Way of Japanese Flower Arrangement Alfred Koehn
Japanese Flower Arrangement in a Nutshell Ellen Gordon Allen
Japanese Flower Arrangement, a Complete Primer Ellen Gordon Allen
Japanese Flower Arrangement Classical and Modern Norman J. Sparnon
The Art of Japanese Flower Arrangement Stella Coe
Sogetsu Notebook for Teachers and Students of Basic Ikebana Joan Lutwyche
Paysages en Miniature Tcheou Tcheng
History of Ikebana Minobu Ohi
The Spirit of the Brush Shio Sakanishi
Sogetsu Textbook Shigeo Suga
The Floral Art, Primary, Secondary and Advanced Meikof Kasuya
Zen in the Art of Flower Arrangement Gustie L. Herrigel
Dried Flowers for Decoration Violet Stevenson
The Eye of the Flower Arranger Lim Bian Yam
Hana kagami Ikebana International, Tokyo

Index